THE OLD PIER, UNION HALL

To Martin

With best wishes.

Paul F.

Martin

Aileen F.

This book is dedicated to the people of Union Hall.

(Up the Haven!)

THE OLD PIER, UNION HALL

PAUL AND AILEEN FINUCANE

Published in 2013 by Red Barn Publishing, Skeagh, Skibbereen, Co. Cork, Ireland

2 4 6 8 10 9 7 5 3 1

ISBN 978-0-9537630-1-6

Project management by Red Barn Publishing, Skeagh, Skibbereen
Printed by Nicholson & Bass, Belfast

Cover: based on a drawing, *The Old Pier At Union Hall*, by Pierce Grace

Contents

Acknowledgements

We are greatly indebted to the many people who helped us in various ways with the production of this book. First and foremost, we are grateful to all of the participating artists for giving so freely of their time, not only in producing a painting but also in providing us with biographical material. In addition, we received invaluable information, advice and encouragement from Patrick Cleary, Ardagh, Union Hall; Averil Cooke, Ballincolla, Union Hall; Jim and Thérèse Gorry, Gorry Gallery, Molesworth Street, Dublin 2; Pierce Grace, University of Limerick; Robbie Limrick, Union Hall; Denis Shanahan, Clontaff, Union Hall; Maura and Malachy Sherlock, Keelbeg, Union Hall; and Tom Skuse, Union Hall.

We wish to thank the National Library of Ireland for permission to reproduce photographic images from its Lawrence Collection for this book.

Dr Ed Walsh, President Emeritus of the University of Limerick and all-round 'renaissance man', very generously wrote a foreword for the book and through his association has hopefully given the book an air of respectability and maybe even an air of importance.

We wish to thank Aidan and Brenda Morris of the Morris Gallery in Skibbereen for their advice and practical help in sourcing local and 'outside' artists for the project. They also photographed many of the paintings in the book and have refused to accept so much as a single cent for all their efforts. We also wish to thank Ben Russell of Kealkill, West Cork, for his outstanding photographic work.

Finally, we wish to thank Brendan Lyons and Gloria Greenwood of Redbarn Publishing, Skeagh, Skibbereen, not only for their professionalism, but also for their advice, patience and friendship through all stages of the project, from conception through to the printing stage. We probably couldn't have done it without you and, even if we could, it wouldn't have been nearly as much fun!

Paul and Aileen

Foreword

It is now over fifty years since I first discovered Glandore Harbour and the island-strewn coast at its mouth; amongst these we fished from small boats and found the best landing places to cook the catch and swim. It was here that I first took Stephanie, my wife-to-be, to sea and afterwards – at 2am the following morning – discovered why her irate father had difficulty in accepting my explanation that the misbehaviour of the Seagull outboard was the sole reason for our late return.

Entering the harbour from the open sea never fails to stimulate. With the local saying in mind – 'Avoid Adam and hug Eve' – one searches to judge the deepwater slot in its unlikely position off Sheela Rock, well west of Adam Island. Onward, past Eve and The Dangers, the scene unfolds to reveal the tranquil harbour above which Glandore's exquisite little church sits, catching the eye as the centrepiece of the cluster of gracious residences clinging to the hill.

After bearing west towards Poll Gorm Bridge and past the old Keelbeg pier, we locate our mooring and, as the boat settles in the flow, sit to enjoy the view of the snug and welcoming village of Union Hall. So we were pleased to learn from Paul and Aileen Finucane of their typically creative plan to commission and publish various renditions of the delightful panorama from their garden over Keelbeg pier towards Poll Gorm Bridge.

I first met the remarkable Finucanes after Paul agreed to accept the University of Limerick's invitation to plan and establish Ireland's first Graduate-Entry Medical School. While our experiences and backgrounds were different indeed, we discovered to our happy surprise that we shared something most important: associations with and affection for Union Hall. My links are less substantial than the Finucanes: they have owned a home overlooking the harbour there for many years, while we have had a succession of boats moored in the middle of it.

It is a tribute to Paul and Aileen's charm, persuasive powers and commitment to the visual arts that such a distinguished group of artists has responded so enthusiastically to their invitation to become involved in this publication. It records for posterity individual interpretations of a West Cork view that must have charmed the many who for countless generations have paused on the very spot to enjoy the vista as the eye follows the water upstream, inland and beyond.

Edward M. Walsh
January 2013

Introduction

Our association with the village of Union Hall in West Cork began over thirty years ago and we have been lucky enough to have a home here since the late 1980s. For much of this time we have been obliged to make our living elsewhere – in such places as Wales, Australia and various parts of Ireland. Even when living overseas, we've always regarded Union Hall as our main home and have gone to great lengths to spend as much time as possible there. Of course, we are not the first 'outsiders' to have discovered Union Hall. Over three hundred years ago, Dean Jonathan Swift liked to visit the area, staying at Glebe House on the edge of the village. It was there that he composed his poem 'The Rocks of Carbery'. More recently, the 1994 David Puttnam film *War of the Buttons* was mostly shot in the village and the surrounding area and captured much of its magic. Aside from poets, prelates and producers, the village and its harbour are also much visited by sailors, holiday-makers and other assorted folk.

The full appeal of Union Hall might not be immediately apparent to the casual visitor. While the village has a wonderful setting on the shores of Glandore Harbour, there are arguably numerous other seaside and inland villages in West Cork and in other parts of Ireland in equally attractive surroundings. With its supermarket, coffee shop, post office, fish shop, two churches and five pubs,

Union Hall Harbour.
Photo from the Lawrence Collection, courtesy of the National Library of Ireland.

THE PIER.UNIONHALL.Co. CORK.10232.W.L

The pier at Union Hall. Photo from the Lawrence Collection, courtesy of the National Library of Ireland.

the village is thriving and quietly self-sufficient. While the multi-coloured terraced houses that line its streets are the stuff of picture postcards, Union Hall is much less photographed than many other villages in the region. It is a vibrant and 'lived in' village. Though essentially in a cul-de-sac, and therefore spared the scourge of passing traffic, there are always people about and it is often a challenge to drive along any of its narrow streets, where cars are often apparently parked at random.

Union Hall is essentially a fishing village and for many generations fishing has been its life blood. Photographs taken over one hundred years ago, for example, show that at that time the harbour and its pier were exceptionally busy, particularly during the herring season. Fish were salted onshore and stored in barrels prior to export. The village provided work not just for fishermen but for fish processors, coopers and sailors. While the fishing industry has seen many a peak and trough in activity since then, it continues to be the most important source of local employment by far.

While acknowledging its spectacular location and interesting history, what makes Union Hall so special for us is its extraordinary community. This is hugely close-knit – a potential source of embarrassment to any 'outsider' foolish enough to utter an uncharitable word about any of its inhabitants. The subject of the insult will surely be a close relative of the person to whom one is speaking. Of course, living in a close-knit community of 200-odd people has its advantages. The residents of Union Hall tend to look out for and look after one another. Even petty crime is all but unknown. Cars are left unlocked, windows are left open and doors are left ajar or on the latch. People come together at times of adversity. The village received national attention in early 2012 when a major drowning tragedy at the mouth of Glandore Harbour claimed the lives of five fishermen. The tireless efforts of the community in searching for their bodies continued for weeks and became a source of national admiration and acclaim. Locals pretty much took this effort for granted – 'Sure, what else would you do?' Over the years, we have witnessed other but less high-profile examples of community spirit on a very regular basis. To us, Union Hall is simply a place apart.

The origins of this book can be traced back to 1995, a time when we lived in Australia. Harry Sherwin, a well-known Australian artist and the friend of a friend, won a travelling scholarship to Europe and visited Ireland. Harry spent a short few weeks in our house in Union Hall and on his return presented us with a small oil painting of the view from our garden. We were totally delighted with this, as it contained an image of the cottage of our good friends and neighbours Maura and Malachy Sherlock, the 'old' pier at Keelbeg and Poll Gorm Bridge in the background. With a typical emigrant sense of nostalgia, we hung this painting in our bedroom so that it was the first thing that we saw on waking each morning and the last thing that we saw on going to bed at night. We brought the painting back to Ireland with us when we left Australia in 2001.

Fast forward to 2006 and to a visit to Union Hall by a dear friend, Murray Edwards, another Australian artist and a near neighbour of Harry Sherwin in the Clare Valley, north of Adelaide in South Australia. Murray stayed with us for a few months and, on his departure, presented us with a painting that he had just completed. By sheer coincidence, this was of exactly the same scene that had earlier taken Harry's fancy. However, the compositions were quite different, as were the media used – Murray worked in pastel, while Harry worked in oils. The contrast between the two paintings gave us the idea of seeing how some local West Cork artists would interpret the same scene. Over the next few years, we began to approach some of them – particularly those affiliated with the Morris Gallery in Skibbereen. The gallery owners – Aidan and Brenda Morris – were a great source of advice and practical help to us in involving such artists as Gus Delaney, Maurice Henderson, Michael McCarthy, Diāna Pivovarova, Martin Stone and Christine Thery in the project. Once we had this critical mass, the project seemed to generate its own momentum.

We approached other local West Cork artists, such as Monica Boyle, Carin Mac Cana, Avril McDermott, Teresa Shanahan and Freddie Sheahan-Murphy, all of whom readily agreed to become involved. During a break from his responsibilities as Artist-in-Residence at the Graduate-Entry Medical School at the University of Limerick, Professor Daniel Duffy visited us at Union Hall and also joined in the fun, thus giving the project even more of an international dimension. We then began to approach some artists whose work we had long admired and, to our great delight, such distinguished painters as Robert Ballagh, Vivienne Bogan, Elizabeth Cope, Martin Gale, John Keating, Arthur Maderson, Una Sealy and Donald Teskey agreed to participate. All of these visited Union Hall at some stage, some managing to stay for just a few hours while others were able to spare a few days or even longer. Just before the book went to press, we were delighted to get paintings from some young and clearly upcoming artists: Alice Rose Clifford, Thérèse Healy-Kelly and Meadhbh O'Donoghue.

The artists featured in this book have come from a surprisingly large number of countries (Australia, England, Hong Kong, Latvia, Scotland, Sweden, USA, Wales) as well as from many parts of Ireland. For us both, one of the most rewarding aspects of this project has been the opportunity to meet with and hear something of the extraordinary life stories of many of the contributing artists. To a man and a woman, they have been a pleasure to get to know and we have already been hugely enriched through the new friendships that we have made. Though they make our own lives appear fairly dull and boring by comparison, we are greatly indebted to each of them for sharing their work and their stories with us.

Most of the pictures in this book have focused on three structures: a cottage in the foreground, the old Keelbeg pier in the middle ground and Poll Gorm Bridge in the background. Their physical relationship is well captured in the line drawing opposite by our good friend Pierce Grace, Professor of Surgical Sciences at the University of Limerick and Chief Clinical Director at University Hospital Limerick. Each of these three structures has of course its own history. Before exploring these, something of the background history of Union Hall might be of interest to readers.

A Brief History of Union Hall

The old Irish name for the village is Bréantrá. This literally translates as the 'Foul Strand' – a name

The Old Pier at Union Hall
by Pierce Grace.

that apparently owes its origins to an ancient sea battle and the place at which the decomposing bodies of those killed, mainly O'Donovan warriors, were washed ashore. It seems that this name was in common use until the early 19th century and is still the official Irish name for the village.

The name change and the more recent history of Union Hall is very much tied up with the impact on the region of the Limrick and Spaight families.

It appears that the Limricks came to Ireland from Scotland in the late 15th century, were based in Northern Ireland throughout the 16th century and moved to the Union Hall area of West Cork in the 17th century. They were aristocrats and intermarried with other local landed families, including the Somervilles of Castletownshend. In 1790, one Colonel William Somerville Limrick, who had retired from the East India Company, built 'a large and commodious dwelling' on the site of an existing hunting lodge. This imposing three-storey house was located at the edge of the village near to the existing causeway. It was initially known as 'The Hall' but had its name changed to 'Union Hall' to celebrate the passing of the Act of Union of Great Britain and Ireland in 1801.

In Griffith's Valuation, which resulted from a survey of County Cork completed in 1853, John Limrick, the son of Colonel William Somerville Limrick, was recorded as owning 'over 8,000 acres in County Cork in the Abbeystrowry, Kilmacabea, Myross and Skull' districts. In 1878, John Limrick's only child, Lucy Margaret, married Colonel William FitzHenry Spaight (1842–1923). The Spaight ancestors were major landowners in County Clare. William FitzHenry Spaight and Lucy Margaret Limrick had four children, the eldest being Colonel Thomas Henry Limrick Spaight, who was born in 1879. The latter Colonel Spaight married Efne Colson in 1904 and in due course inherited 'Union Hall' and the many dwellings belonging to the estate. The Spaight family lived in the village intermittently until 1922, when the big house was burnt down by the IRA and the ruin later demolished. While the Spaight family never returned to Union Hall thereafter, there are still many Limricks living in and around Union Hall.

'Sea Pie' Cottage

Local opinion is that this cottage and the smaller cottage to which it is attached were built in around 1840 as coastguard residences, two of a number of such residences in the immediate vicinity of the old pier. It was constructed from the same stone that was used in the walls surrounding 'Union Hall'. The cottage was sold by Colonel Thomas H.L. Spaight to Margaret Skuse in 1947 and has since been owned in turn by the Glenton (1964–1971), Phillips (1971–1973), Doyle (1973–1985) and Sherlock families. William (Bill) Glenton was a former *Daily Mirror* journalist who sub-let a room in his London docklands home to his friend Anthony Armstrong-Jones (later Lord Snowdon) for his secret trysts with the late Princess Margaret. In 1965, Bill Glenton published a book, *Tony's Room: The Secret Love of Princess Margaret*, which told the story of that relationship. The book was apparently written while he lived at his cottage in Union Hall. Along the way, the house acquired the name 'Sea Pie Cottage'. The present owners, Malachy and Maura Sherlock, have now lived there for almost thirty years.

Keelbeg Pier

The 'old pier' at Keelbeg dates from sometime in the late 19th century. In 1885, the then local newspaper the *Skibbereen Eagle* advertised for a contractor for its construction. Colonel Thomas H.L. Spaight once wrote a family history in which he stated:

> The stone pier at Keelbeg was built when I was a schoolboy; until then all sea traffic for the

village used to come up to our private quay below the house. The coal schooners which sailed across direct from South Wales used to deliver their cargoes there for old Mrs Fuller, whose store contained all the necessities of life including peppermint bullseyes for ourselves and all that was needed for making up our fishing tackle.

As Colonel Thomas Spaight was born in 1879, this implies that the pier was built in around 1890, and certainly before the turn of the 20th century.

It is clear that the pier made a crucial contribution to the local economy throughout the 20th century. Photographs from the Lawrence Collection taken in the late 19th and early 20th century show some very large boats docked at the pier, with others moored offshore. For decades, locally caught herring were salted near the pier prior to export – often to Russia to help feed its army. The old pier also served the sizeable local fishing fleet until the construction of the new pier nearby in the early 1990s. Keelbeg pier also saw action during the Irish Civil War (1922–23) when the Public Armed Ship *Muirchú* (formerly the Royal Navy ship *Helga*) landed Free State troops at Union Hall in an attempt to outflank local Republican forces. The *Helga* had been involved in shelling Liberty Hall from the River Liffey during the 1916 Rising and was later used to transport British Auxiliary troops (the 'Black and Tans') around West Cork during the War of

Independence. The *Muirchú* sank off the Saltee Islands in County Wexford in 1947.

In recent decades, and particularly since the construction of the new pier nearby, the old pier has been allowed to fall into disrepair, particularly at the seaward end. Nowadays, it is mainly used by some smaller fishing boats and occasionally by visiting yachts. In the summer, local children (of all ages) fish from the old pier and use it as a diving platform.

The Bridge

The single-lane Poll Gorm Bridge, which connects the Aghatubber and Ardagh townlands, derives its name from a large pool of water on its northern side that never dried up and was known as the 'Poll Gorm'. The bridge was built between 1885 and 1887 – at around the same time as the stone pier at Keelbeg. It is an all-steel structure and is supported by steel piles screwed directly into the seabed. The construction materials were brought on three steamers from Stockton-on-Tees in north-east England and assembled locally. It took two years to complete the work. In his family history, Colonel Thomas H.L. Spaight states:

I remember the building of the iron bridge across the harbour to replace the old wood-bridge that was there. I wonder whether it still has the official notices on it giving warning of the safe loads that it could carry . . . in Irish at one end and in English at the other.

PIER.UNIONHALL.Co.CORK.5221.W.L.

The pier at Union Hall. Photo from the Lawrence Collection, courtesy of the National Library of Ireland.

It seems safe to assume that the notice in Irish would have been at the Union Hall side of the bridge, as Union Hall has always had a more 'native' population than the more anglicised village of Glandore.

The present bridge was preceded by a low narrow wooden bridge, which was 600 feet in length and was built in about 1862 at a cost of £3,000. This bridge had an unhappy history, due, it seems, to its poor construction. Just three or four years after it was built, at a meeting of the County Grand Jury – the forerunner of the County

Council – in 1866, it was stated that the bridge 'had so sunk that it was almost impassable' and it was agreed to allocate an additional £400 for its thorough repair. At that meeting, it was stated that the bridge had 'three times the traffic of the Kinsale bridge'. Despite the additional expenditure, the wooden bridge lasted for little over twenty years in all. It could be raised to allow large boats to access the upper reaches of Glandore Harbour and the village of Leap. To this day, the approach slabs of this original bridge remain intact and some of its timber stumps can be seen near the present bridge just above the waterline at extreme low tide. Before the wooden bridge was built, a ferry boat connected the two sides of the harbour, travelling between Scully's strand in the townland of Ballincolla (Place of the Ferry) and the small boathouse directly opposite on the Glandore side. For over one hundred years the Poll Gorm Bridge has been the principal route of access to and egress from Union Hall to the east and continues to be very heavily trafficked, particularly in the summer months.

So much for the history of Union Hall and the landmarks that feature in the paintings contained in this book! As this project of ours developed, we have been fascinated by the way in which the different artists have interpreted the subject material. As far as possible, we have tried to be non-prescriptive and to allow the artists to deal

The harbour at Union Hall. Photo from the Lawrence Collection, courtesy of the National Library of Ireland.

with the task as they saw fit. Specifically, we have not given an opinion on the medium to be used, on the size of the painting or even on how the finished painting might best be framed. None of the artists had the opportunity to see the work of others in advance. All were assured that they were not involved in a competition, that all paintings would be valued and that diversity in the approaches taken would be looked on as a virtue rather than as a vice. Some participants took 'artistic licence' and painted a scene that was sometimes a little and other times a lot different to the one which we had suggested. We had no problem with this, understanding that artists tend to work best when they engage with a subject that interests them. Of course, not all of those who we approached agreed to become involved, while some of those who initially agreed clearly struggled with the subject matter and either failed to complete a painting or to deliver it to us.

With regard to the biographical statements, in the main these were put together following a single interview or a series of interviews with each artist. We then drafted a biographical statement based on what was said to us and this was sent to the relevant artist for approval or for changing. Nothing has therefore appeared in any biographical piece without the knowledge and consent of the person concerned. Apart from the one sketch that was written after the death of the artist Murray Edwards, all pieces are written in the first person, as this was how the material was given to us. As far as possible, we tried to capture the 'turn of phrase' and something of the character of each artist in the biographical sketches. The approach taken was designed to ensure some degree of uniformity in the book while hopefully avoiding a 'formulaic' approach.

We hope that this collection of paintings of the pier at Keelbeg will continue to grow in the years to come. At some stage they will also need to find an appropriate permanent West Cork home.

Paul and Aileen Finucane
Union Hall, November 2013

Robert Ballagh

on marriage. However, I don't think that he ever really warmed to Catholicism. My mother, Nancy Bennett, was a descendant of the Westropp-Bennetts from Limerick. My maternal grandmother was a Smithwick and was related to the Kilkenny brewers. Both of my parents were elite athletes. My father played cricket and tennis for Ireland and rugby for Leinster. One of his Leinster caps is still in the family. My mother played hockey for Ireland and I have a team photo from 1938, when she played against Germany in Köln, where the German players are giving a Nazi salute. I was an only child and inherited none of my parent's athleticism.

I recently stumbled upon the fact that I must have family connections with Union Hall through my Westropp ancestors. I now know that a certain Colonel William FitzHenry Spaight was responsible for changing the name of the village to 'Union Hall' in 1801. The Spaight and Westropp families were intermarried – for example, Thomas Spaight (William FitzHenry Spaight's great-great-grandfather) married Elizabeth Westropp in 1684 and their son William married Anne Westropp (presumably a cousin of his) in the late 1730s. When the Spaights later moved to West Cork, they intermarried with the Somerville and Limrick families, so that I probably share quite a bit of my DNA with the Somervilles of Castletownshend and the Limricks of Union Hall.

Anyway, to get back to my own upbringing, Ballsbridge in the 1940s and '50s was a very

As was commonplace in the early 1940s, I was born in a nursing home – one on Pembroke Road in Dublin's southern suburbs. I was brought up on Elgin Road in Ballsbridge – where the US Embassy has since been built. My father, also called Robert, was raised a Presbyterian but converted to Catholicism

different place to what it is today. While I would describe ourselves as a 'lower middle-class' family, we had no money. At that time, everybody was poor. My father did a lot of voluntary work for St Vincent de Paul and he would bring me with him when he visited the poor of the locality. I'll never forget the poverty of those living in Turner's Cottages on Shelbourne Road. The floors were of clay and the children went barefoot. I'm told that when the US Embassy was planned for Elgin Road, questions were asked in the US as to why it was being built in a slum area. However, despite the general poverty, I felt privileged to grow up in this environment.

Before primary school, I went to Miss Meredith's, which was something of an institution in Ballsbridge. While this was predominantly a girls' school, it did take boys up to primary school age. I then went to St Michael's on Ailesbury Road, which was then tiny and run by the Holy Ghost Fathers as a preparatory school for Blackrock College. In due course, I went to Blackrock, where I was mentored by a wonderful art teacher, John Coyle. I studied art with John as a Leaving Certificate subject. The emphasis was on still-life drawing and we would all sit around drawing bottles and the like. John recognised my talent, tapped me on the shoulder one day, led me to a separate table and from then on I was able to work on my own pictures under his tutelage. Despite this, art wasn't of any great interest to me at that time; like other youths I was more interested in kicking a ball and playing tennis.

Any embryonic interest that I might have had in art was eclipsed one day in the 1950s when my father brought me to the Carlton Cinema in O'Connell Street to see Bill Haley in *Rock Around the Clock*. Rock music became the real passion in my life for several years. Somehow or other, I saved £5 to buy my first guitar. My friend Alan Devlin and I formed a band and Alan's father Johnny, who was a professional musician, gave me guitar lessons. After school, I would go to another friend's house and listen to records of Chuck Berry, Fats Domino and Jerry Lee Lewis. At the age of 16 or 17, we were playing regularly at local tennis clubs, and thought that we were wonderful but were probably awful.

As my schooldays were coming to an end, I saw an ad in the *Evening Herald* for a bass guitarist in a band. Just as I agreed to sign up, and in the best Irish tradition, the band decided to split. I went on with one of the offshoots to form The Concords. We were semi-professional and could play just about anything. Depending on the audience, we could move from rock 'n' roll to céilí music at the drop of a hat. It was a great learning experience. It also introduced me to the Trade Union movement, as, early on, I was stopped from going onstage at Dublin's Olympic ballroom one evening because I wasn't a union member. I had to do an audition to be allowed to join the union.

At this time, I also started to study architecture at Dublin's Bolton Street. I would have preferred art school, but my mother wouldn't hear of this as she couldn't see it leading to a proper job. She would probably have supported me in anything other than a career in art. In this, she might have been influenced by the death through suicide of a cousin who was a talented artist. For me, architecture was a reasonable compromise. I enjoyed my time at Bolton Street, where I was exposed to some inspirational and talented tutors. For example, Robin Walker (later of Scott Tallon Walker) had just come back from Chicago, where he had worked with Mies van der Rohe, having previously worked with Le Corbusier in Paris. Donal McCann worked at the drawing board next to mine and we became lifelong friends. Donal went on to become one of the greatest actors that Ireland has ever produced. However, he had his demons and was a martyr to the drink. For three years, I managed to combine my studies with work as a semi-professional musician. Then one day, I returned from a gig in Derry to face into my end-of-year exams in Bolton Street. I fell asleep at the exam and failed the year. Rather than repeat the entire year, I decided to quit and become a full-time professional musician.

Through the 1960s, I was bass guitarist with the Chessmen Showband. The story of the Irish showband phenomenon hasn't yet been told and this needs to happen. Ireland was changing rapidly at this time and the country's dance halls were a harbinger of this change. In 1959, Seán Lemass succeeded de Valera as Taoiseach and worked with T.K. Whitaker in dragging Ireland into the modern world by removing the tariff walls that had suffocated the country. Up to then, Ireland's isolation had included the arts: there were no cultural imports and just about every worthwhile book, play or film was banned. I think that Lemass and Whitaker planned to open up the country's economy but to keep everything else the same. This, of course, turned out to be impossible. In rural Ireland in particular, the showband scene was part of a cultural revolution. We would arrive in some out-of-the way place in our gold lamé suits, looking as if we'd been parachuted in from Las Vegas, to play before an audience who were still living in the '50s, with cow shite on their boots and the like. We were well aware that we were part of something new and were very excited by this. Over time, popular demand meant that rock 'n' roll music gave way to Country & Irish and I never liked this. After a four-hour gig one night, I realised that I hadn't played a single number that I'd liked and so I decided that it was time to move on.

Showband work was well paid, so, when I quit at the age of 23 or 24, I had enough in reserve to do nothing for a while. By then, I'd met Betty, who was a few years younger than me. We used to drink in Toners in Merrion Row, where the artist Tim Goulding was a mutual friend. Tim was responsible for my next job. Another artist, Micheál Farrell, had returned to Dublin from New York, was looking for an assistant and approached Tim, who declined but suggested me instead. At our first meeting, Micheál asked me: 'Can you draw a line?' He then offered me £5 a week as his assistant and 'all the drink you can take'. He was working on a National Bank of Ireland commission and Ardmore Studios in Bray was the only place big enough to accommodate the work. I was still living at home, while Micheál was renting a huge ramshackle house (complete with ballroom) in Killiney. I would collect him from there in the mornings and drive him out to Bray. Peter O'Toole and Katharine Hepburn were filming *The Lion in Winter* in Ardmore at the time. We all had great fun.

I then headed for London, where I lived in South Kensington with some old friends from Bolton Street. I later realised that Francis Bacon

4   THE OLD PIER, UNION HALL

had his studio (now reconstructed at the Hugh Lane) next door, but I was unaware of this at the time and never met him. Betty had moved with her family to Manchester and later joined me in London. One fateful evening in 1968, we decided that we'd get married, would move back to Dublin and that I'd become an artist. Of course neither of us had a job, we had no place to live and had spent all our money. While my mother was tearing her hair out, neither of us were at all bothered by this. Anyway, we rented a bedsit in Rathgar and borrowed my mother's car to go to the Aran Islands on honeymoon. Betty's mother, Molly, also came to our aid. Though she'd moved to Manchester, Molly still held the tenancy of her old Dublin home in Broadstone. She encouraged Betty and I to live there and we later bought the house for £750. This was no small amount of money at the time, but we were able to borrow from friends and parents. Some forty-five years later, I'm still living in our Broadstone home.

The one thing that I was qualified to do was to draw and I got a job as a draughtsman, earning £20 a week, or £16 after tax. Here again, I quickly found myself embroiled in trade union rows and had a crash course in industrial relations. This was a boring job and I was only able to stick it for nine months. Through a friend of my father's, I then got a job designing stick-on labels at 30 shillings per design and this gave me a bit of income while freeing up time for painting. Then, in the early 1970s, the Department of Posts and Telegraphs asked me to design a postage stamp. In this way, I was able to ease my way into being a full-time professional artist. The fact that I was doing something quite different attracted early attention

and allowed me to build a reputation. I was once referred to as Ireland's best 'pop artist', but it was easy to be the best when I was really the only person doing this kind of work. At the age of 26, I had my first solo exhibition, in Brown Thomas on Grafton Street. This was in 1969, the same year that I was invited to represent Ireland at the Paris Biennale. It was also the year that our first child, Rachel, was born. Our second, Robert, was born in 1975. To distinguish him from his father and grandfather, Robert was immediately nicknamed 'Bruce' and this name has stuck. Rachel is an artist and Bruce works in the motor car trade.

In the late 1980s, I was one of a dozen artists invited to enter a competition for the design of a new Irish banknote. This was a Central Bank initiative that aimed to make forgery more difficult. Though I initially struggled to come up with an idea, something finally clicked and, to my great excitement, I won the competition. Beyond the design, initially I hadn't much of a clue about what was involved. A bank note is a security document rather than a work of art and production is a very complex process, taking at least six months to produce an engraving from the design. I was fascinated by the collaborative nature of the project and it was a joy to be involved. Work on a £20 note led to work on other denominations and, as they were all produced in Germany, I was over and back to Munich on a regular basis. The notes that I designed were in use for ten years, until the introduction of euro banknotes in 2002. Over the years, my involvement with stage design has also pushed me out of my comfort zone. This work dates back to 1985, when the theatre director Michael Colgan

View from the Bedroom; oil on canvas; 2013; 105 × 97cm.

asked me to design a stage set for a Beckett play at the Gate. In 1994, I took on the stage design for *Riverdance* and my long association with this has allowed me to travel the world, while providing me with a degree of financial security.

I often reflect on the fact that I've been very lucky throughout my career. One of my major faults – an inability to say 'no' – has often worked to my advantage in surprising ways. Out of a sense of desperation, my wife Betty would regularly threaten to send me to a tattoo parlour to have the word 'NO' inscribed on my forehead. The inability to say 'no' also got me into my fair share of scrapes. In 1991, for example, I attended a public meeting in Liberty Hall that was held to plan an adequate celebration of the 75th anniversary of the 1916 Rising. I had no intention of getting involved but ended up as Chairman of the 'Reclaim the Spirit of Easter' event that ensued. This led to derogatory statements about me in the Dáil and to telephoned death threats. While all of this now sounds so silly, the death threats were particularly unpleasant at the time, especially with kids in the house. However, out of it all came the so-called 'Hume–Adams initiative' and a public debate in Dublin's Mansion House, where Gerry Adams was first provided with a platform. I also received an apology and a sizeable settlement from the *Sunday Times*, which I sued when it accused me of being an advocate for the cultural wing of the IRA or some such. This was a strange time indeed.

We are again living in a very strange time, in the aftermath of the collapse of the Celtic Tiger. Nobody seems to be talking about the real issues. While I'm no economist, I have a passion for democracy, equality and justice. With an accumulated debt of €600 billion, it's clear to me that we have no hope of even keeping up with interest repayments. In crucifying the Irish people, the government is being told by the IMF and others that it is doing a great job. Everything is being decided behind closed doors by non-elected people in Europe. Why is the establishment so contemptuous of democracy? Why is it such a bad thing to give people a voice? How have we arrived at the ridiculous situation where sovereign governments in Greece and Italy have been removed and replaced by non-elected technocrats?

After the wretched winter of 2012–13, I'm thinking of going to someplace warmer next winter to try and write something for a change.

2

Vivienne Bogan

and old women chatting outside little shops, carrying bundles of firewood beneath long black shawls, Mrs Hanley's kindergarten school and Stella cakes with Grand-Aunt Rita. The week's highlight was the Sunday morning parade, with me best positioned on the top floor waiting expectantly for the music. The Boherbuoy Brass and Reed Band, St Mary's Fife and Drum Band or another of Limerick's best, marching in all their regalia down O'Connell Street. I still thrill to the sound of a live brass band.

My parents met while working at Shannon Airport. My mother, Mary, was with TWA until she married, while my father, Robin, worked for Pan Am until the airline left Ireland in the 1970s. When I was aged 7, we moved to the suburbs and to a garden where my mother could fulfil her dream of growing flowers. I found new friends and the wonders of freedom in roaming the nearby fields. At 11, I discovered my first love – the stage – and performed little plays and concerts for neighbours and even had a go at *Hamlet*. Later, shyness and self-consciousness prevented me from pursuing this love. A seriously exciting event in my young life was spending a month in Long Island, New York, at the age of 12. This was the start of a lifetime of travel. Arriving in downtown Manhattan in the swinging 1960s – Warhol was somewhere nearby – was a total culture shock coming fresh from de Valera's 'dancers at the crossroads'. There, I had my first official art class, drawing dancers at the New York Ballet Company

My first view of the world was from the third-floor windows of my parents' flat on Limerick's main street in the grey 1950s – an inner-city childhood with the sounds and smells of industry. Early memories are of daily walks in People's Park, playing under the austere gaze of Thomas Spring Rice atop his Doric column, wandering home on dusky evenings with the smell of coal smoke in the air

THE OLD PIER, UNION HALL

in rehearsal. This is still a vivid memory and had a profound effect on my subsequent life.

My father's ancestors were shipbuilders in Barnstaple, north Devon. On the other side of my family, my maternal grandmother, Ethel Hederman, was an amazing, gregarious and inventive woman and a huge presence in my young life. She had that great hospitality, curiosity and general receptivity so typical of people of that era. She loved to paint and encouraged me to do the same and her praise helped to counteract the constant battering to my self-esteem that I received at school. Then, joy of joys, that September day when, after much debate with my father but with support from my mother, instead of returning to secondary school I entered the Limerick School of Art & Design. At that moment the world began for me and I started on the endless journey of learning and discovery under the mindful but relaxed guidance of the principal, Jack Donovan. The 'huge' intake of twenty students spent idyllic days sampling a variety of art disciplines and hanging out in the White House pub. Of course, exams were done and teaching qualifications eventually awarded, but all this was intertwined with trips to places like Argentina, Alaska and Bali, courtesy of Pan Am. I had summer jobs in the US, Bermuda and Australia, was a parish priest's housekeeper in Chicago and sold all things 'Western' in San Francisco. My parents were wonderfully relaxed about me wandering off alone, even providing me with a round-the-world ticket at the age of 20.

I returned to art school to concentrate on painting and printmaking and, with guidance from master printmaker Dietrich Blodau, qualified some six years after starting. The 1970s and '80s saw a blossoming of the arts. Galleries were opening and there were exhibitions and invitations to 'open submission' shows. I taught and painted continuously and showed my work wherever possible. I had my first solo show at Dublin's Project Arts Centre and the next at Ciaran McGonigal's Grafton Gallery. I later moved to the Riverrun and then the Hallward Gallery and had my work included in prestigious shows, including the Oireachtas, Living Art and EV+A.

My marriage to Andrew Bromfield, a lecturer and translator of Russian literature, meant a return to the travelling life. An academic year in Glasgow was fun but, the following year, painting and exhibiting in Yerevan, Armenia, was just splendid. The opportunity to see at first hand the ancient art, architecture, people and cultures of Central Asia, including Azerbaijan, Uzbekistan and Turkmenistan, was amazing, as little had changed down the centuries except for the ubiquitous symbols of soviet occupation.

The impending arrival of our son, Kolya, brought us home and his sister Robyn's appearance two years later kept us there. Back in the Irish art scene, I worked at 'All Plus 10 Sorts' studios in Limerick, exhibited where possible and received a Guinness Peat Aviation award and a couple of Arts Council bursaries. Believing it important to give something back, I worked on the EV+A Committee and served for five years on the Arts Council. I was then off again, this time for ten months to idyllic Cyprus and later for two years to central Moscow at the time of Glasnost and Perestroika. Here, there was little food and surviving on rubles was difficult. Andrew translated while I painted and taught

Terra Incognita; mixed media on synthetic gauze and paper; 2013; 58 × 54cm.

English at a Japanese school, our children struggling with the soviet education system. Their schooling eventually became a priority, so I returned home. I again painted, taught and exhibited when possible and also returned to the Limerick School of Art for a 'refresher' year. I joined Contact Studios and Limerick Printmakers. For the past fifteen years, I've had the hugely rewarding experience of working on a variety of arts and dance programmes with adults with learning difficulties, through the Daughters of Charity. I now live in East Clare, where I have my own studio. My works are in various public and private collections, including those of the Arts Council, the Office of Public Works, the Office of the Revenue Commissioners, Allied Irish Banks, Shannon Development, the University of Limerick, Mary Immaculate College, the Council of Europe, the Musée des beaux-arts de Quimper, Brittany, and the office of the Spanish Prime Minister.

I don't regard myself so much as a painter but as somebody who enjoys using all sorts of materials – fabrics, wood, my own stitched and dyed hand-made paper, found materials, etc. – in attempting to make visual something of the 'unknown self' in inks, pastels and paints. Like my materials, my subject matter varies according to outside influences. Very often nature and my environs (e.g. land or cityscapes) dictate. At other times, the excitement of the accidental and the resulting Alice in Wonderland-type adventure is what's needed. I'm attracted to the fascinating but challenging demands of portraiture, and the spirituality of the creative process is hugely important to me. The meditation and prayer that is creativity has assisted me through many troubles down the years, helping me to re-establish tranquillity, self-confidence and grounding.

Visually representing the inward explorations that we all once undertook as children provides me with the little jewels with which I've decorated my life and which keep me striving to unearth brighter and more exciting gems. Down the years, through all the trials, tribulations, triumphs and travels, art has been my one constant, my one dependable reality. These words of T.S. Eliot aptly synopsise my philosophy of life:

We shall not cease from exploration
And the end of all our exploring
Will be to arrive where we started
And know the place for the first time.

Mine is a life of journeys and explorations, of reaching outwards to fascinating people, places and encounters but equally to those curious worlds within. I strive to get a glimpse of and grapple with Freud's 'cauldron of seething excitement' – the chaos of the unconscious mind. My aim with art is to grab something of life, to try to put it out there, to endeavour to make it visible.

3

Monica Boyle

*Photograph by
Fiona Brophy*

I was brought up in the Scottish village of Duntocher in Dunbartonshire, about 9 miles west of Glasgow. I am one of a family of nine, which includes two sets of twins. My mother, Sarah (Sadie) Murray, was born of Irish parents in America but moved to Scotland at the age of four. My father, James Boyle, worked for Rolls Royce and throughout his working life was heavily involved in the trade union movement. My parents had a very strong sense of social justice, which they passed on to their children. With such a large family, money was scarce, but what we lacked in resources we made up for in creativity. One of my earliest memories is of my mother manufacturing makeshift paintbrushes by trimming the ends of

her long black hair and sellotaping it to pencils to occupy us on a gloomy, wet afternoon, much to the fascination of the visiting district nurse. As children at play, necessity forced us to make our own toys, dolls, sling-shots, racing carts, tree houses and dens of every description, using whatever materials we could find. I think that this inventiveness and understanding of materials is vital for artists, but unfortunately it is lost to today's generation of children.

At school, I did well academically and was therefore compelled to study Latin and denied the chance to do art, which I would have much preferred. By the end of my schooling I was drawn to creative writing and did a Media Studies course at Glasgow Caledonian University in Glasgow. At the same time I became involved in a community outdoor project in Dunbartonshire, working with primary school students and family groups from disadvantaged areas. This was more in keeping with the value system with which I had been brought up and, not surprisingly, I subsequently swapped journalism for community education, initially on a voluntary basis during my summer holidays from college and later on a full-time basis. A key component of the outdoor project involved taking groups to the Inner Hebrides for the summer months. Over time, I began to spend longer periods there and developed a fascination with islands and with island life. I met my husband, Paul Perry, on the Isle of Eigg. He had been sailing in the Caribbean and came to Eigg as

A Winter-Seeming Summer's Night; diptych; oil on linen; 2012; 25.5 × 60cm.

a ferry-boat driver. We later lived together in Gloucestershire, where I worked with the Wildfowl Trust as an education officer. Increasingly, arts and crafts became a significant tool in my work. I then studied Youth and Community Development in Leicester, but, whilst this was enjoyable, I desperately missed living by the sea.

As a teenager I would often escape the 'liveliness' of our house by walking for miles along the nearby River Clyde, where the scenery looking west to Loch Lomond and the Trossachs is quite beautiful. I thus developed a fascination not only with rivers, the sea, shorelines, piers and bridges but with abandoned docks and derelict industrial yards that smelled of diesel and dirty water. Subsequently, I produced whole series of paintings based on these subjects – piers in particular. I have even used materials sourced from these neglected places (e.g. bits of rope, rust and netting) in my work, in an attempt to make paintings that evoke such places and that are, literally, like the subject itself. I enjoy the sensuality of paint, its physicality, texture and smell, the way it smudges and smears, and also that a finished painting documents the process and progress of the work – in other words, every mark that the artist makes is recorded in the finished product, as though set in concrete.

We moved to West Cork in 1990, partly because some of Paul's extended family members were already living in the area. We initially set up a gallery in Baltimore, but this venture was probably ahead of its time and we soon abandoned it. The arrival of our three girls, Amelia (b. 1994), Sophie (b. 1996) and Sadhb (b. 2000), kept us busy for a while. I started taking life drawing and painting lessons with Peter Perry and Terry Searle, while at the same time running a play group in Baltimore, which I did for eleven years. I loved working with young children – their imagination is boundless – and the art work that I did with the group helped my personal development as an artist. In 2001, I was accepted on a pilot BA course in Visual Art being offered by Dublin Institute of Technology on Sherkin Island. This was meant to be a five-year course, but problems with accreditation and course funding meant that I wasn't able to graduate until 2010. During a four-year period when the course was suspended, I showed with Cunnamore Galleries, which was owned by Chris Boon and Diana Pitcher. I learned a great deal from Ian Humphreys and John Simpson, who were always generous with their extensive knowledge of painting and exhibiting. At the same time, I had several solo exhibitions and participated in group shows in various venues, including London's National Theatre – a great privilege for someone as inexperienced as myself.

I paint almost exclusively in oils and most of my work is landscape-based, much of it centred on Heir Island. On my first visit to Heir, I had a strong sense of having been there before and I became completely enchanted with it. The atmosphere on Heir is completely different to any other of the West Cork islands; there is a timelessness that seeps into my paintings. In the early phase as a career artist, I mostly painted Heir from a distance. Later, I began going over on the post boat, before there was a regular ferry, and so painted the interior, developing a relationship with the island's residents in the process. We often stay there in the summer, sometimes camping, and we like to swim there. Many people consider my paintings of Heir to be melancholic and it is true that I have used them to explore aspects of chiaroscuro (the contrast between light and dark). The paintings are also quite 'tonal', without a huge range of colour. I suppose that this aspect of my work can be traced back to my Scottish origins and the Scottish fascination with the 'gloaming' – the transition between day and night. My work also explores the interface between land and sea, the past and present, absence and presence, the real and the imagined.

The historic aspect of painting is important to me and I enjoy the craft of constructing the supports for my paintings and don't mind spending time on this. I make my own stretchers using traditional methods and materials, for example using rabbit-skin glue to seal the canvas. I use lead primers if I can afford the time that it takes for these to dry. I paint mostly on linen and, even when I use board, I generally glue linen on to it. I mostly source my raw materials from a number of long-established art suppliers in the UK. I'm an impetuous person and the process of sizing and priming my canvases slows me down, as does working in oil. With oil, you sometimes have to wait weeks for paintings to dry. Afterwards, I tend to flood my paintings with layers of dilute paint, which introduces an element of chance and accident. I like to apply paint and wash it off again to see what's left behind. This also gives my works a patina and makes it difficult to place in time.

Looking back on the way that my life has developed over the past few decades, there has always been an apparent dichotomy between my life as an educator and as an artist, but, in reality, each has fed and encouraged the other. I have always struggled to accept painting as a career, as it seems an inherently more selfish and self-indulgent occupation. I continue to teach and I regard this as my 'giving back' time; however, I realise how much art means to me and to other people and that it is a real privilege to be an artist.

4

Alice Rose Clifford

I was born in 1993 and raised around Tulse Hill in south London. My Mum, Liz McDonald, is originally from Castleconnell, a small village near Limerick, and studied medicine at University College Cork. She now works as a Consultant Perinatal Psychiatrist in Hackney, east London, where she helped set up a unit for women experiencing mental illness during pregnancy and after childbirth. My Dad, Paul, is also a doctor, who, having started out as a Clinical Psychologist, now directs a company developing analytic software for health and social care. He is expanding his business in the US and so currently splits his time between America and our home in London. I'm the youngest in a family of three. My middle sister, Anna, has just graduated from Trinity College Dublin with a degree in English and Music. My eldest sister, Aislinn, works in London as an animator, among other things.

I went to the same London school for fourteen years – from the age of four until I sat my A-levels. I considered leaving for my final two years, as it was a very high-pressure environment, but I ended up staying on, mainly because of the fantastic art department. My A-level subjects were Maths, Physics, Art and Art History. It was an odd mix, which made it difficult to decide on what to do next. I'm now studying Physics at Bristol University, where I'm in the second year of a four-year Master's programme. I'm pretty unsure of what I'll do when I finish; there are so many options out there and I'm very indecisive by nature. At the moment I'm interested in the whole area of patents and patenting and might end up as some sort of patent attorney, as I like the idea of spending all day trying to get to the core of other people's ideas. This seems like a good way around the difficult task of combining science with creativity.

Whereas I have only become interested in physics in the last few years, art has always been a passion. My mum tells of how, when I was very little, I announced that when I grew up I wanted to be an 'outdoor artist', which I suppose is what I'm doing now. If I could make a career out of it, this

ARC

THE OLD PIER, UNION HALL

would be perfect. When I was younger I would go to the home of an artist named Peter Aswood on a Saturday morning, where we would do everything from painting and drawing to papier-mâché and crazy wire sculpting. When I started secondary school I was mainly taught to draw from observation. I couldn't be more grateful to my teachers from those early years, as it's a skill I won't forget and simple pencil drawings are still my favourite thing to do. Second to that I love to paint, either very intricately using gouache or larger paintings in acrylic.

Towards the end of my school career, and in particular on leaving school, my confidence got thoroughly knocked and it was a long time before I got back into drawing again. I'm now enjoying this more than ever and have recently moved into a room in Bristol which is big enough for me to set up my easel. I take weekly life classes and haven't ruled out the possibility of going to art college after I finish my Physics degree. However, it's definitely too early to plan that far ahead and, if I'm honest, I think I would rather carry on creating art on my own, without the pressure and guidance of an institution.

My family has been coming to West Cork since before I was born. When I was very little we'd go to the White Houses in Baltimore every holiday, and for a few years we rented a cottage in Tralispeen belonging to our London neighbours, the O'Keeffes. We eventually built a house near Lough Ine nearly ten years ago. My childhood memories of West Cork mainly involve swimming, kayaking and horses. We all swim year-round, even participating in the Christmas swim at Tragumna with not a wetsuit in sight. I suppose West Cork

lost some of its attraction for me in my early teens, but I still enjoy coming over for a week or so with friends in the summer and we've had some nice Christmases there, even if they were a bit quiet.

Over the last couple of years I've been able to explore Europe more, as I've been old enough to travel alone and with friends, and I've seen some beautiful art. I've always loved Robert Delaunay's brightly coloured geometric paintings – my seventeenth birthday present was a rare edition of a book on him and his wife Sonia – so being able to see his paintings at the Guggenheim in Venice was amazing. Before that, I'd only seen one painting by him – of the Eiffel Tower – at an exhibition at the Tate in London. My favourite contemporary painter is the London-based artist Lee Maelzer; I think she creates the most beautiful paintings of odd and often banal scenes.

Over the years, I've used all sorts of media in my drawing and painting. I mostly draw with pencil but have worked with most things. For A levels, we had to use a variety of media and I used to enjoy using chalk pastels. I mainly paint using acrylics – I've considered switching to oil paints but I use my hands a lot in my painting so I worry about what the oil and thinners would do to my skin. I apply the paint initially using big brushes then form the image with my fingers and palms. I use my bare hands a lot to form an image.

My favourite subjects to paint and draw are people and, given a choice, I would just do this all the time. However, trying to find people who are willing to sit for me isn't always easy and I don't enjoy painting from photos. I've spent a lot of time painting from still life, which I enjoy to an extent but sometimes find quite limiting. More recently

Untitled; acrylic on board; 2013; 117 × 122cm.

I've moved more towards landscape painting. Although I have often created abstracted images, I've never made a completely abstract work. When I was first asked to produce a picture of Union Hall for this book, I thought it was a fun idea, though having never seen the scene I wasn't sure of what to expect. I came over from Bristol especially to work on the painting, which took me two days to complete. For the first day I worked outdoors, as I felt too detached from the scene when painting through a window. However, I was unlucky with the weather and had several incidents where the painting and easel blew over completely, so I stayed indoors the next day. At one point the fog was so thick that I could hardly see beyond the end of the pier and couldn't see any of the Poll Gorm Bridge. I didn't intend to make such a large painting – I had bought half a standard block of MDF and planned to cut it down after making the painting – but I found it surprisingly difficult not to fill the whole space. After I'd finished, it was interesting to see the approaches taken by some of the others who've contributed to this book.

I've never really had my work exhibited, other than at school. There must be hundreds of my paintings stored at home or at the houses of friends and family. Aidan Morris at the Morris Gallery in Skibbereen has offered me an exhibition for next year, so hopefully I'll find time to produce enough work to get exhibited, although it will definitely be a challenge to achieve this alongside a Physics degree.

5

Elizabeth Cope

I was brought up in the village of Ballitore in County Kildare. My father, Michael Lawler, was a talented sportsman and musician who at different times worked as an undertaker and dairy farmer. My mother, Dora King, was a very beautiful woman, also from farming stock. After marriage, she ran a grocery shop in the village, selling celebrated ice cream as well as our own milk and vegetables. She married at 20 and had nine children. As the middle child, I was close to all of my siblings. I attended the convent school in Athy and then won a horticulture scholarship to An Grianán in Termonfeckin, County Louth, but only stayed a week. To please my mother, I did a shorthand and typing course, which led to a job

with a Dublin television rental company and this allowed me to attend the College of Art in the evenings.

When I was 9, a sister brought me a box of Chinese oil paints from Paris and I really was seduced by the smell of the paint, although it was ten years later in my Dublin bedsit that I made the conscious decision to become a painter. I moved to London, initially working for an advertising agency in Piccadilly and teaching art and other subjects at a Kensington prep school. In my spare time, I attended the Sir John Cass School of Art in Whitechapel (now part of London Metropolitan University) and took singing lessons from Elizabeth Fleming on the Brompton Road. Living in London stimulated my cultural appetite and I would go without food to attend a ballet or opera. I was once lucky enough to see Margot Fonteyn and Nureyev dance at Covent Garden. I then spent three years at the Chelsea School of Art, working part-time to pay my way. I sold ice cream in Hyde Park, cleaned toilets in a Knightsbridge hotel and sold pencil portraits in St James's Park. I became an au pair to escape a gloomy Shepherd's Bush bedsit and sold Greek Island holidays by phone.

The only useful things that I learned at art school were how to stretch canvases, the use of models and other facilities and how to sculpt from clay, cast in plaster and make etchings. Art schools should be banned! In the main, they are staffed by mediocre artists and can be very cruel to young

View from Upstairs; oil on canvas; 2013; 59 × 73.5cm.

THE OLD PIER, UNION HALL

people. You need to be mature and have had some life experience to survive.

I returned to Ireland after six years, making ends meet through part-time teaching and art sales. I met my husband, Geoffrey Cope, when I taught at the Carlow Vocational School, where he was a student. During our early years together we lived in various places including Paris, where I painted and worked as an au pair while Geoffrey taught English. We married in 1980 and our three children arrived in due course. Phoebe is a painter and sculptor. Reuben is a film-maker, a sculptor, a painter, an installationist and a clown (like his mother), while Sybil is an archaeologist. Since 1991, Geoffrey and I have lived at Shankill Castle in Paulstown, County Kilkenny, together with our cattle, ducks, geese and several donkeys. The castle was once a Butler tower-house but has been modified repeatedly over several hundred years. We open both the castle and its gardens to the public during the summer.

I regard myself as an expressionist/ impressionist painter. I like art that irritates, not in the sense of creating an annoyance but like the grain of sand that upsets the oyster to make a pearl. A piece should draw me visually into an emotional arena and translate into an emotional response. Art should hurt by touching something a bit raw. Otherwise, it is just so much decorative wrapping. With too much formalism, work can become dry and sterile. I always need to find the emotional base, letting emotion leak into the painting without being afraid of self-exposure. For me, art without an emotional base does not work and art that doesn't work comes out of a design aesthetic. Too often the aesthetics of design contaminate the making of art. Like a pathologist performing an autopsy, the artist is both involved emotionally and yet detached from the work, so that the act of painting is both passionate and dispassionate. As a child I wanted to be a nun and saint, like St Thérèse of Lisieux. I soon realised that this wouldn't happen, but hoped that becoming a painter might allow me to be a 'second-rate' saint. This was all before I lost my faith when I became ill, but that's another story! I believe that the dedication of a painter allows a spiritual freedom and I see painting as a kind of prayer that lifts the spirit from the mundane. Everything we do in our personal lives must be sensitive to all people around us. One cannot but be aware that even the mundane can have its political implications.

I like colour and movement in my work and often draw and paint while subjects are moving about. I paint very quickly. I've tried slowing down to see what this is like but find that, being fluid and sloppy, oil paint needs to be worked quickly. I paint in a subconscious way, without thinking too much about the component parts of the activity or the end product. If I can achieve this spontaneity, it is like being in a state of grace. I have both made the painting and not made it; it has merely happened. By nature I'm an improviser and need to be inventive in my painting, as in other aspects of my life. I'm always keen to try new ways of seeing. I love to draw and sculpt and hope to make more sculptures in the future.

I mainly paint in oil and don't like acrylic, the smell of which reminds me of dirty socks! I love painting outdoors, but, while I'm not an easy studio painter, I've disciplined myself to work indoors. Unlike writers, who can keep warm while writing in bed, our climate doesn't help painters. Still, for me nothing beats painting in a ploughed field on a sunny, cold and frosty winter's morning. Wind is my great enemy; I can easily cope with rain and snow. I have painted in the streets of London and Honduras and from the back of a truck in Somalia. I like to paint from life, particularly the nude model. I'm intrigued by the physiology of things, both plant and animal. Regarding other painters, I particularly admire the work of Velasquez and Matisse. For me, Jack Yeats has been Ireland's best painter by far, due to his great feeling for colour. Francis Bacon's early work was brilliant, but his later work became too slick. Bacon would surely laugh at the idea of a peeping hole into his re-created studio.

Despite the chaos of life, I work every day if possible. Over the years, I've exhibited extensively in solo and group shows throughout Ireland, in the UK (London, Edinburgh), in Europe (Paris, Brussels, Bologna, Zurich), in the US (New York, Chicago, Boston, Florida, Dallas) and in Mexico City. This information can be found on my website: <elizabethcope.com>. For me, the subject matter is only an excuse to paint. It's irrelevant whether you use people, interiors, places or still-life objects as subject matter, it's all painting in the end – just as putting on one's socks could be regarded as a political statement! With my work, I try to make the viewer feel something and to make myself feel something. I feel there is no other reason to engage in art practice. Painting helps me find out what my real central concerns are. My pictures have taught me that concision, but not constriction, is essential. After a forty-year apprenticeship, I like to think that my perception of myself as a painter is expanding.

6

Gus Delaney

I was born in Cork city on 29 April 1940, the eldest of two children. My mother, Mary (née Hassett), originally came from Millstreet in north Cork and was a schoolteacher, while my father, William, worked in agrochemicals. I was educated at Christian Brothers' College (CBC), University College and the College of Commerce, all in Cork. My professional speciality was in secretarial practice, company law, human resources and, principally, financial management. I had a long association with the employers' body IBEC and for a time served as its Cork regional president and on its national executive. All of this commercial activity commanded most of my attention until my retirement in 2002. I have spent most of my life in Cork city, where I now live with my wife Jeannette and my daughter Amy. Jeannette and I have three other daughters – Martine, Yvonne and the late Karen.

For as far back as I can remember I have been involved in drawing and painting and in handcrafts generally. In my earlier years I had some tuition from the now Galway-based artist Kenneth Webb and the now London-based Professor Anne Tallentire. At that time, both artists were very much part of the Irish school of landscape painting and their teaching sessions provided valuable exposure to the approach, the modus operandi and the underlying dedication, competence and commitment required of a professional artist. There have been others since who, to varying degrees, have further contributed to my enjoyment, artistic style, execution, education and improvement.

I have painted throughout my adult life but, because of the time demands of business, this of necessity could only be infrequent. Having retired as the Chairman and Chief Executive of a multinational corporation in 2002, I had the time to focus on my lifelong interest in painting. Initially, post-retirement, I found watercolour to be a most exciting and my preferred painting medium. To my mind, it enabled competent subtlety of expression and development of tone

Union Hall, West Cork; acrylic on canvas board; 2011; 22 × 29cm.

and colour to a satisfactory and aesthetically pleasing and rewarding extent. I painted numerous watercolours at this time, as the wide appeal of and the demand for my finished works was matched by my personal satisfaction in producing them. My own pleasure originated entirely from the execution and presentation of a pleasing (to me) work of art and I also welcomed the vote of confidence in my work when it was accepted for display by many local art galleries in the initial years. I have long believed than many people would value owning an original painting but might initially be daunted by its cost. I have therefore always pitched my work at a modest price in the hope of demonstrating their easy availability and affordability, either for a person's own consumption or as a unique/original gift for someone special.

Following this initial watercolour period, I gravitated towards painting with acrylics and, unlike some other artists, became increasingly comfortable with the versatility, flexibility and vibrancy of colour achievable with acrylic paint. However, as the subject matter dictates, I still work in watercolour from time to time. While some prefer the purity of pastel and others choose to work in oils, I continue to achieve much satisfaction with acrylics – even given my wont to turn out very detailed paintings at times. Other than when commissioned to represent a specific subject, I tend to paint mostly landscapes or buildings that relate to a specific place. All of my work could be regarded as figurative and none ever gravitates towards the abstract. I have my work double-mounted by a professional framer in Cork and I prefer to see my paintings under glass if and when being framed. I no longer routinely frame paintings, because overseas buyers cannot easily transport glass and because most buyers prefer to choose their own frames to suit their home décor.

Over the years I have completed a large number of commissions, as many who have viewed my work tend to look for a painting of their own place rather than some subject which has appealed to me. When considering work to be shown in a gallery or otherwise, I have found that viewers tend to be more interested in local scenes and subjects. My Union Hall painting in this book is one of the more unusual commissions that I have undertaken. In late 2011, I welcomed the invitation to participate in a rather unique and unusual challenge: to paint a garden foreground and inner sea inlet at Union Hall and in due course to be compared with others who would be similarly directed was curiously appealing. This for me was all the more interesting because my family and I spend a lot of time at our holiday apartment overlooking the inner harbour and town of Kinsale, with its several famous landmarks and forts. In this location I am continually fascinated by the ever-changing moods of the sea at different times of the year.

I continue to get pleasure and satisfaction from the reaction of people to my work and welcome the many constructive suggestions that are offered from time to time. Such input can also contribute to variations on a theme which can sometimes make the outcome far more attractive to the viewer. Over the years many friendships have developed with those who have bought my work in various places and I have enjoyed receiving letters of thanks and compliments (all of which I keep) from far and near. I particularly recall an English lady who purchased one of my paintings in a Skibbereen gallery to remind her of her visit to Ireland. She later wrote me the most beautiful letter of thanks and commendation and has since commissioned four other paintings of places that mean a lot to her. Each Christmas she writes to say that she continues to get great pleasure from seeing my work on the walls of her home.

None of the foregoing can take from the fact that I regard myself as a 'hobby' painter and continue to enjoy that role. Whether a painting sells or not is less relevant than the fact that I enjoyed painting it. I can do no more than offer it for sale at an affordable price, donate it to charity or give it as a gift to friends and then leave the judgement of value to the recipient. The notoriety that sometimes accompanies the work of other artists has never had any appeal whatsoever for me. My justification for painting rests entirely on the pleasure my work can and has given to others and the satisfaction that it has always given to me.

I have a keen interest in where my work ends up and am therefore aware that my paintings are on display in private homes in several parts of the globe – in the USA, Germany, France, UK, Norway, etc. – and continue to be in demand as gifts and as mementoes. I am a member of the Maclise Art Society in Cork and have often exhibited with them over the years. I look forward to and regularly attend the painting demonstrations and competitions arranged by the society each month in the Crawford Art Gallery in Cork.

Looking to the future, I think this will probably involve a continuation of my painting activity as at present. Most who pursue a painting pastime seem to reach an older age without any interruption of their interest and with an on-going inclination to improve even further. This certainly applies to me.

THE OLD PIER, UNION HALL

7

Daniel Mark Duffy

I am a first-generation Irish-American and was brought up in Summit, New Jersey, USA. My father, Eugene Aidan Duffy, came from Trim, County Meath, and emigrated to the US when aged 14. He first lived with relations in Summit and in 1957 married my mother, Barbara Jean Coppo, a nurse from Paterson, New Jersey. They raised their family of six in a small suburban home in New Providence, New Jersey. I was the third born. We all attended the local elementary school, where my third-grade teacher, Ms Babcock, first recognised and nurtured my artistic potential. At the age of 11, I began to attend the New Jersey Center of Visual Art, where I studied drawing, painting and sculpture. I developed quickly and, aged 14, won the Fine Arts gold medal at the New Jersey Scholastic Olympics. The solitude that I craved in our crowded home I found instead in the woods and along the banks of the nearby Passaic River, and so drawing became my way of escape when at home or in school.

At the age of 16, and with the assurance of teachers and the blessing of my parents, I entered the Hoboken, New Jersey, atelier of the American artist C.N. Jones III to study classical painting and drawing. Two years at the easel rendering casts and methodically building small still-life paintings in oil, together with visits to NYC museums and galleries, were transformative. I built a portfolio, which in 1979 led to a scholarship to the Pratt Institute, a large private art college in Brooklyn, New York. I spent three semesters at Pratt, but,

Low Tide; oil on canvas; 2012; 39 × 49cm.

eager to explore other landscapes, I left art school and instead spent six months painting in Ireland. I then moved back to Hoboken and set up my first studio. In 1981, I received an Emerging Artist Award from the National Society of Arts and Letters and established a relationship with my first art dealer. At this time, I also attended master classes with the famous American artist Philip Pearlstein. I began to accept portrait commissions and mounted my first solo exhibition of urban and rural landscapes in Hoboken in 1981.

New work being exhibited in Soho in the early 1980s challenged my perception and commitment to the classical tradition and so, at the age of 22, I decided to return to art school. I received a scholarship to the Carnegie Mellon University in Pittsburgh, where I majored in painting and art history, studying with the artists Sam Gilliam and Herb Oldes and the art historian Edith Balas. There, I was able to experiment with scale, alternative media, textures and narrative, allegorical and symbolic imagery. No longer willing to spend endless hours defining observed subjects with meticulous detail, I painted with abandon, letting the paint defy reality. My work involved large surfaces, big brushes, pouring and splattering thin or thick acrylic or oil paint, adding waxes, sand and photographic images. After graduating with a Fine Arts degree in 1987, I first moved to Jersey City Heights, New Jersey, and was then selected from over four hundred applicants as science illustrator in the Department of Vertebrate Paleontology at the American Museum of Natural History, New York. In 1989, I began to accept freelance illustration work, mostly of book covers, children's books,

movie posters and advertisements. My work was included in the Society of Illustrators' annual exhibition in 1991 and 1994 and the children's books *Molly's Pilgrim* and *Theodoric's Rainbow* received national awards.

In 1990, I married Mary Jo Limpert, who is an actress and singer. We first settled on the Upper West Side of Manhattan, where I balanced my time with commercial art projects, portrait commissions and painting, printmaking and photography. Our place became too small with the arrival of our daughter, Áine Elizabeth, in 1997, so we packed up the baby and three labrador retrievers and moved sixty miles north to the small rural town of Newtown, Connecticut – the place that I still call home. In 1998, I was commissioned to paint the portrait of the then Dean of New York University Law School, John E. Sexton. This led me down a path of painting commissioned portraits of several senior academics from Ivy League and other universities, of Supreme Court and other judges and of high-profile politicians, including New York Governor Andrew Cuomo, Vice-Presidential candidate Jack Kemp and four former US Cabinet secretaries.

When in my early 40s, I was appointed Adjunct Professor of Fine Arts at Paier College of Art, Hamden, Connecticut. The human figure remains an integral part of the curriculum at Paier College and my work with models and students inspired a series of paintings and drawings on which I continue to work to this day. A year after my appointment at Paier, I received an unusual commission to paint a nude portrait of a woman who found my work on the internet. This prompted me to approach American women of mature years to pose for a portrait unclothed and I found that many were quite happy to do so.

As a young boy, I spent many summers in Ireland and developed a particular attachment to my maternal grandmother, Molly Keating, whose transcendent beauty and dignity informed my perspective, inspired a career in portraiture and educated me on the significance of history. I travelled a great deal through Ireland as a teenager, have always felt at home here and had the honour of becoming an Irish citizen in 2007. Most of my father's family still live in that part of County Meath where he grew up. I spent the summer of 2007 with family in Trim and wandered the streets of Dublin photographing decaying areas that the Celtic Tiger was preparing to raze. The ageing human portrait theme that I had explored at Paier began to re-emerge in my mind. I began to reach out to Irish women whom I had come to admire and whose history captured some unique part of the nation's character and this soon become my primary focus. Such women included the actress and Oscar-winner Brenda Fricker, the journalist and women's rights campaigner Nell McCafferty, the singers Mary Coughlan, Frances Black and Honor Heffernan, and the artists Camille Souter, Maria Simons-Gooding and Imogen Stuart. The art dealer Isobel Smith, actors Olwen Foure and Kate O'Toole, author and environmentalist Judith Hoad, Castle Leslie Estate owner Samantha Leslie, archaeologist Carmel O'Byrne with her four daughters and National Archives Director Pat Donlon all became involved.

The portrait of Nell McCafferty, the first of the series to be exhibited, was included in the Royal Hibernian Academy 2008 Annual Exhibition, where it received major media attention. It featured in all the national newspapers; Nell was interviewed on radio and the portrait was unveiled on the *Late Late Show*. A photograph of the painting taken by Brenda Fitzsimons was included in the *Irish Times*' 'The Year in Pictures' for 2008. The portrait was one of 49 selected from over 5,000 submissions for the 2009 Outwin Boochever Portrait Award Exhibition at the Smithsonian Museum, National Portrait Gallery, in Washington. In 2009 I exhibited a series of nude drawings at Dublin's Tramyard Gallery and was included in the Davy Portrait Award exhibitions at Queen's College in Belfast, Farmleigh House in Dublin and Fota House in Cork in 2008 and 2009. My work has featured in the RHA Annual Exhibitions of 2008, 2009 and 2012; the latter included a portrait of Sir Jack Leslie, cousin of Sir Winston Churchill. In 2011 I was awarded the first Lundbeck Fellowship in the Humanities and Art residency at the University of Limerick Graduate-Entry Medical School. I am currently completing my series of nude portraits of mature women, which will be exhibited in Dublin and in New York in 2014.

8

Murray Edwards

Murray was a man of many talents and very many graces. Not only was he a highly accomplished painter and a potter, he was a qualified teacher and also something of a philosopher. Born in Sydney, Australia, at the outbreak of World War II in 1939, he was christened Robert Murray and was the second of four children of Norman Edwards and his wife, Una Everingham. Murray considered his father (also a schoolteacher) to be a singular influence in his life. He has written of a 'wonderful childhood and adolescence in country towns and in the beautiful Blue Mountains [west of Sydney]'. He began drawing in early childhood and won his first prize for drawing at school at the age of 11.

In the late 1950s, Murray trained as a teacher at Bathurst Teachers' College in New South Wales, where he studied art as an elective subject. Some fifteen years later, he obtained a BA degree in English and History from the University of New England, Armidale, also in New South Wales. He then led something of a nomadic life as a teacher and for over thirty-five years taught in various primary and high (secondary) schools in New South Wales, Queensland and South Australia. This included a period working with the Flying Art School in Queensland, a job that involved the promotion of the visual arts in rural and remote parts of Australia. During this time, he spent three years training as a potter while continuing to develop his skills in drawing and painting.

Above Sancta Maria – Union Hall, Co. Cork; pastel on paper; 2006; 28 × 35.5cm.

Murray married Judith Bingham in 1963 and the couple subsequently had three children, Charles, Steven and Megan. Their marriage ended in 1982, at which time Murray moved to Brisbane, where he continued to teach. His transition from a schoolteacher to a full-time artist took off at about this time and he began to exhibit regularly in solo and group exhibitions in various parts of Queensland. In the mid-1980s, South Australia was at the forefront of the arts in Australia, while Queensland was still something of a cultural backwater. This at least partly explains why Murray moved to the wine-producing Clare Valley, north of Adelaide in South Australia, in 1986. There, he continued to teach part-time while immersing himself in South Australia's vibrant art scene. He began his second long-term relationship, with Christine Alway, in 1987 and a daughter, Rowena, was born to the couple in 1995.

In 1988, Murray moved to Corella Hill, a delightful 38-acre property near the village of Watervale in the Clare Valley. Here he had 'magnificent views into bushland gullies and over the patterns of vines on rolling hills, nestled in a grove of Blue Gums and Red Gums [eucalyptus trees]'. It was here that he built his mud-brick studio and gallery in 1991. Following a trip to Scotland – the home of his ancestors – in 1992, he decided to resign from teaching and devote himself to full-time painting. The studio struggled initially and Murray later talked of how he 'lived on the smell of an oily rag' at this time. Happily, this state of affairs didn't last. The Clare Valley and its vineyards is a major tourist destination in Australia and Murray's studio soon became a popular venue, particularly at weekends and holiday periods. Those who regularly visited Murray at Corella Hill were generally as much attracted to the man as to his work. Soft-spoken, witty and engaging, he took a great interest in people and always made his visitors feel welcome and valued.

The late 1990s represented a difficult time in Murray's life. In 1997, he developed cancer and all that went with this and, two years later, his second long-term relationship came to an end. He painted little around this time but resumed painting again in 2000, taking a refresher course in the Central School of Art in Adelaide in 2001. Following a short few years of relatively good health, his cancer returned in 2003 and he never really regained full health thereafter. Nevertheless, he was well enough to visit Ireland in 2006, when he spent a few months in Union Hall with his daughter, Rowena (then aged 11), who attended the local national school. During this time, Murray felt quite fit and energetic and painted regularly. Like many an artist before him, he marvelled at the light and the volatility of the West Cork climate. He took a particular delight in painting fuchsia, stating that 'native fuchsias line the lanes around Union Hall – they are so beautiful, going perfectly with all that is green. I will remember them for years to come'. Sadly, this proved not to be the case. His health again deteriorated and just five years later – on 24 October 2011 – Murray died at home at his beloved Corella Hill in the Clare Valley.

Murray had his first one-man show in Queensland in 1985 and subsequently exhibited in numerous one-man shows and group exhibitions in South Australia. He was a strong supporter of and regularly exhibited with the Clare Valley

Artists Group. He won several awards for his work and is represented in corporate and private collections throughout the world. He painted in a very distinctive style, such that his work is instantly recognisable. While he was skilled in all media, in the later stages of his career he worked mostly in pastels, and he described how he applied them 'heavily in rich and intense colours in a spontaneous, energetic and impressionistic style'. Clare Valley landscapes were a favourite theme – particularly the contrast between vineyards in leaf and the brown soil. He retained his drawing skills and complemented his landscapes with life drawings. He claimed that his work was 'more involved with concepts, moods and personalities of things than with realism' and that his work 'reflects the credo that art without passion is art without life'. Among his major influences were Marc Chagall, Vincent van Gogh and Claude Monet, the Australian artists Lloyd Rees, Brett Whiteley, Arthur Boyd and Ivor Hele, and the American poet Robert Frost. During his time in West Cork in 2006, he became totally captivated with the paintings of Christine Thery (who has also contributed to this book) and whose work he considered to be 'up there with the best of them'.

Apart from painting and drawing, Murray loved to travel and, among other places, spent time in India, Nepal, Italy and Greece. He regarded his visits to Scotland and Ireland as among the greatest experiences of his life. Among his other interests, he listed rowing, bushwalking, gardening, archaeology, reading, cooking, theatre, poetry, philosophy, psychology, yoga, steam engines and single malt whiskey. He summed up his goal in life as 'wanting to make the world a better place'. Those who knew Murray are in no doubt that he succeeded in his life goal through both his art and his humanity.

9

Martin Gale RHA

I was born in Worcester, England, in 1949 to an English Catholic father and an Irish Protestant mother. Though originally well off, both sides had suffered reversals earlier in the century. My mother's family (her maiden name was Shepherd) had made a lot of money in Canada in the 19th century and had moved to Eyrecourt in County Galway at the beginning of the 20th century. However, the Wall Street crash of 1929 wiped them out and my mother's education was cut short; she returned from school in Wales to help run the stables at home. My father came home from the war and took out an amateur riding licence. He had a few years of steeplechase racing until he met my mother and they married. He turned professional the year that I was born and for ten years we moved around between England and Ireland, as he was attached to different stables from year to year. My brother Dermott was born in Cork a year after me and we grew up together. We were educated partly in Ireland and partly in England and then sent to boarding school in Ireland.

Both sides of the family had a more than passing interest in painting. I still have a terrific watercolour painted by an aunt of my mother's while the family were still in Canada. My father's mother was a very good painter, though being from the 'horsey' world she mostly painted portraits of people's horses, usually on a commission basis. My father also painted very well, though not often enough. When we went on family holidays, he brought his painting materials along and had usually produced a painting by the end of the week or fortnight. We were always encouraged to draw and paint as children and I suppose that is where my interest in painting began. After leaving school, I got a job in Rank's flour mills in Phibsborough, Dublin, as a trainee something-or-other – a manager, I think! Within a year I had applied to the National College of Art, ostensibly to study graphic design, but, once I discovered the school of painting, that was it really.

My time at art college from 1968 to 1973 was a time of major turbulence and student unrest. We spent a lot of time either sitting-in or locked out. The Department of Education had little interest in the college; the fees were £22 10s, which tells you

Sighting Australia; oil on linen; 2012; 40 × 50cm.

something! Although at the time it was something of an educational backwater, the college still turned out some fine artists and art teachers. My contemporaries included such painters as Michael Cullen, Charles Tyrrell, Brian Maguire, Gene Lambert, John Devlin, Michael Mulcahy, Mary Farl Powers, Liam Belton and several more. One of the first and most important things you learn in art college is how to see – really 'see' – the world around you. Once you have acquired that skill, it never leaves you.

With the arrival of pop art in the 1960s, fine art and applied art sort of merged and our visual awareness was heightened. Images appeared everywhere, on shopping bags and LP covers; there was an explosion in poster design. Everything was on the hop and anything seemed possible. It was a great time to be coming out of art school. I remember having two paintings selected for the Irish Exhibition of Living Art in 1972. It was a major breakthrough for me at that point. I was canning peas in Essex at the time and, as soon as I learned that both paintings had sold, my pea-processing career came to an end! Shortly after that I had a two-person show in the Davis Gallery in Capel Street with fellow student John Devlin. The following year my graduation show was seen by Bruce Arnold, who was running the Neptune Gallery in South William Street at the time. He took me on and in 1974 hung my first one-man show.

Around that time, my wife and I moved to West Wicklow, where we rented a cottage and had three children. With the demise of the Neptune Gallery in 1980, I moved to the Taylor Gallery and have been with John and Pat ever since. The kids, Jonathan, Rebecca and Robert, are all involved in the arts in one way or another and have each been incorporated into my paintings at some point over the years. In 1980 we moved to Ballymore Eustace on the Kildare/Wicklow border, where I still live and have a studio. The going was tough for a while – I drove a school bus for a few years – but then in 1981 Aosdána was established. An annual stipend of £4,000 was a huge help, allowing me to concentrate fully on painting.

I paint in oils and watercolour, concentrating on one painting at a time. I occasionally get involved with printmaking at the Graphic Studio in Dublin, but really my main focus is on painting. People often ask me where the ideas for paintings come from. The answer is anywhere and everywhere. Often a painting will develop from the previous one and so on, especially if I happen to be working on a series. Sometimes a place will become the starting-point for a painting and I can use it as a foundation on which to build a possible narrative. On another occasion it might be a person or an event that kick-starts a process that hopefully will lead to a painting. Once the various ingredients have been decided upon and assembled, the business of making the painting begins. I usually start by doing small watercolour studies, then perhaps a small canvas, working out composition details, etc., and hopefully solving any problems that may crop up before going on to work on the larger picture. This period is important, because it can save a lot of strife and chopping and changing during the final painting. Of course, nothing is really final until the painting is completely finished. Hiccups, changes of mind and various unforeseen twists and turns can occur any time during the work on the picture, but good preparation reduces the risk of things going wrong in the middle of the whole thing.

My paintings are 'realist', in that they deal with the visible world. They often carry the suggestion of a possible narrative, but nothing is spelled out. They are usually landscape-based, but there is often something else going on, or at least the suggestion of a situation. I believe it is essential to leave space for the viewer to bring something to the painting. If the possibility for the viewer to participate in the interpretation of the work is absent, then I feel the painting has fallen short. My paintings are often described as having 'an edge' and I suppose this is the case sometimes.

I was elected a member of the RHA in 1996 and have since served as Keeper for eight years. In 2013, it was my great honour to be awarded an honorary docorate by NUI Maynooth for my services to the arts in Ireland. Throughout my career, I have exhibited widely in Ireland, England, Europe and the US and my work is now held in many important public and private collections. The RHA hosted a major retrospective of my work in 2004/5 and this later moved to the Ulster Museum in Belfast. However, like many other artists, I believe my best work lies ahead of me. As Picasso said when in his nineties, what kept him painting was the fact that he still had so much to learn.

THE OLD PIER, UNION HALL

10

Thérèse Healy-Kelly

imaginable. Orla is the eldest in the family; then come my twin sister Mary and I, followed by Siobhan, Tim and Kate. Tragedy, however, did intervene with the death of my beloved brother Tim when he was just 21 and of my much-loved Aunt Peggy when I was also at an impressionable age. The emotion and depth of feeling surrounding such losses often come to the surface when I hold a paintbrush. My Aunt Peggy was a great lover of art and she and my parents encouraged this interest in me from a young age. Others in the family had musical talents, but, being tone deaf, as a child I instead had art lessons, from my Aunt Agnes in the nearby town of Buttevant. Early on, I was appointed official artist to our family, for example being given the job of producing a card for our Nanna's 80th birthday. This turned into a long-standing annual commission, as Nanna survived well into her 90s. In other ways, I was constantly called upon to draw and paint while the others played away on their fiddles, flutes and pianos.

I worked hard on my art during my years at the local convent school in Kanturk. I was inspired to fill my work with vibrant displays of our country life; these were magnified through the imagination that only a child can conjure. I experimented with colour and portraits and was the child in the classroom called upon to draw for the school magazine. I took Art as an extra subject when I sat the Leaving Cert in 1990, a year of much change. The Berlin Wall had come hurtling down and the

I'm a '70s baby and was reared on the family farm at Rossacon, a few miles from Kanturk, among the rolling green fields of North Cork. I'm the joint second child in a family of six. Our father, Conor Healy, and mother, Noreen (née Noonan), worked hard and gave selflessly in ensuring that we all had the most idyllic childhood

Untitled; oil on canvas; 2013; 60 × 45.5cm.

THE OLD PIER, UNION HALL

liberation of Eastern Europe was at hand as I left home for University College Cork. College life brought a new sense of liberation and thoughtfulness that moved my work in a more introspective direction. I was fascinated by the temporal relationship between people and their environment, including images of modernity juxtaposed with stillness. In my art, I returned to the images of farm life and the light that clearly permeates every facet of life in the open.

I graduated three years later with a degree in Economics and Maths and with all the positives of a university experience. Completion of a Higher Diploma in Education led to teaching jobs in Dublin's Tallaght, in Fermoy and in Tipperary town, where I mostly taught maths, business and enterprise studies. The long summer holidays allowed me to travel and, in the space of a few years, I was able to get to London, Australia and the US, all of the time eating up whatever the art world had to offer. Museums and galleries were my addiction and I began to seriously consider pursuing a career in art. I left teaching, studied computer programming and had a short career with a software engineering company. When I met and later married Jack Kelly, my computing career came to an end and my travelling began in earnest. Jack is a plastic surgeon and our early years together were spent in Melbourne, in Texas and in the UK. Melbourne was a busy time for me, in that I taught, took classes in watercolour at Flinders College and had our first child. We now have five children: Isabelle (b. 2002), David (b. 2004), Hugh (b. 2005), Zack (b. 2007) and Amelia (b. 2009).

Following stints at Galveston, Texas, and in Oxfordshire, we returned to Ireland in 2004 when Jack took up a consultant post in Galway, and where we have lived since. I particularly enjoyed my time in Oxford. I soaked up its history as best I could and also travelled regularly to London to visit its art galleries. Happily, Jack also has a strong interest in art. We both love living in Galway and greatly appreciate its absorbing sense of everything cultural. There's a great appreciation for the arts in all its forms here. That stated, the arts have suffered in Galway as elsewhere in the past few years; some significant city-centre galleries have closed and the lack of a major public art gallery in the city is a huge deficiency.

I've studied art wherever I've lived – in North Cork, Melbourne, Galveston and now in Galway. At Galveston, I studied under Sally Anderson and developed my technique with watercolours. Here in Galway, I've been greatly encouraged by Miriam Cronin at her 'Paint Box' studio in Barna. I'm also enrolled in a degree course in Art and Design at the Galway-Mayo Institute of Technology (GMIT), where Dermot Delargy is just one of the many inspirational tutors who help me to develop a deeper understanding of critical theory and art history. The portrait work of Colin Davidson, Ewan Uglow and Una Sealy and the still lifes of Giorgio Morandi and Brian Ballard never fail to inspire and move me. Having used a range of media over the years, I now prefer to work in oils. I seldom paint outdoors, not only because of the ever-present wind and rain on Ireland's west coast but also because of time constraints.

My subject matter comes mostly from the everyday life that I lead with my husband and children. I have painted numerous portraits of the children. They are all quite musical and Isabelle's involvement with a youth orchestra stimulated me to produce a series of paintings of musicians. Even our dog, Juno, gets in on the act and a painting of him at the end of the stairs is a nod back to my rural upbringing and memories of my father's dog. I love to paint city life and Galway street scenes – the winding Shop Street and Quay Street – and also the city dock and nearby coastline. The trawlers gathering along the city docks and their reflection in water have the same fluid quality of oil on canvas board as it drips and captures by itself the life and feelings of the scene. I'm an emotional painter and, while my work has a prevailing emotion of happiness, it contains a bank of all feelings. I feel happy while I'm painting and I hope this is reflected in my work, as it's the emotion that I want to evoke in the viewer.

Though I dream of establishing a full-time career from art, my main preoccupation just now lies in the creation of a loving home with my husband and five kids. Both Jack and I lead pretty hectic lives, so that painting has to fit in between rearing my kids and running a bustling home. We are currently renovating our 1830s home, and setting up a studio/gallery there is part of the plan. I paint to relax and to unwind in the evenings when the kids are in bed. When not painting, I'm constantly thinking of what I'll paint next, for example in looking at the play of light on water and thinking of how I might capture this in a painting. Over the past few years, I've exhibited with the 'Paint Box', have briefly exhibited at Dublin's Lyndsay Gallery and have been an invited artist at the Kanturk Arts Festival exhibition 'Hinterlands'. I'm currently working towards my first solo exhibition.

11

Maurice Henderson

I'm a war baby and was born in 1944 near Farnborough in Hampshire, England. World War II brought people to England from many countries, including my father, Gordon Fry, who came from Canada and met my mother, Kathleen Doyle, at a local dance. They married and moved to Calgary in Canada, where my younger sister, Beverley (now a highly regarded portrait painter), was born. The marriage was a disaster and, like many other war brides, my mother returned to England with her children. Memories of my childhood in Canada are strongly negative and life back in England wasn't much better. We lived with my widowed grandmother in Farnborough, together with an aunt and two uncles. Even at the age of 7, I was acutely aware of the total poverty in which we were living. To me, post-war England was awful – as if everybody was dead or missing – and I was only able to understand the tragedy of the situation in my later life.

Although my mother was a staunch Catholic, I went to a local Church of England junior school, which provided me with both food and friendships. I joined the Boy Scouts and greatly valued the adventures and companionship that this provided. When I was 11, my mother married James Henderson, who was an army officer. Although I took the Henderson surname, we never were able to become the family of which my new father dreamed. I was sent to a Salesian College, an experience for which I can never find forgiveness. The pain ended when I got a scholarship to Farnham Art School and my life began to finally head in a good direction.

I experienced both highs and lows at art school. I remember a day in my second year when the school principal came to assess the students' work. I had painted an old graveyard scene and, in appraising this, the principal referred to me as 'an artist' while all the others were referred to as 'students'. At the time, I was as much shocked as honoured and wished that I had had the foresight to leave school at this stage and follow my own path. Shortly thereafter, the curriculum changed completely, moving away from figurative art towards abstract expressionism and

Union Hall Harbour; oil on canvas; 2012; 48.5 × 59cm.

constructivism. Graduates were encouraged to have a commercial focus and to embrace technology. I struggled with this and my work became the subject of derision rather than praise. I finally moved to London's Goldsmiths College, where I obtained an art teacher's certificate. However, on graduation I was unable to find a teaching post.

A chance winter holiday in West Cork in 1973 exposed me to its beauty and persuaded me to relocate, in an attempt to recapture my love of figurative painting. At that time West Cork was totally unspoilt and life was simple. Food was basic and affordable, milk came from a neighbour, bread was baked in a bastible over a turf fire and there was an oil lamp for the evenings. In reality, life was never quite so idyllic but it was nearly perfect in its own way. Despite an initial lack of self-confidence, constant fights with depression and a lack of medical and financial support, I began to fulfil my dream of painting. I was able to support myself with sales, with prices ranging from £12 to £75 for oil paintings. Solo and group shows followed, both locally and nationally. Other artists came to West Cork and I had hopes of establishing a network of artists who would support and encourage one another. However, personalities, competition and egos got in the way and this ambition of mine has only ever been realised in my dreams.

Slowly, West Cork began to change. Electricity and television arrived and a passing car was no longer a novelty. At the same time, the reality of living obliged me to focus on money as much as on art. My son Orion was now at school in Cork and needed a home to provide a sense of belonging. I borrowed enough to secure an old house badly in need of repair but with a roof, windows and a garden. Money had to be made for the loan repayments and, on occasion, I submitted as many as seventy watercolours to shows in Dublin and Cork. In summer I made the occasional sale to passing tourists and somehow it was possible to keep going.

I had been very involved in the anti-war and other protest movements in London in the 1960s and later took an interest in the Irish anti-nuclear movement. In the 1990s, my work took on an anti-war and anti-imperialism theme. For a Nuclear Awareness Project I produced hand-made books consisting of torn sheets of wrapping paper, collages of photos and coloured shapes. Most of the images alluded to the atom bomb, nuclear testing and war paraphernalia, coupled with photos of African tribal people and images of babies in the womb. I decided against using text, as this would open up the books to personal interpretation. With support from the Arts Council, the books were featured in a major exhibition of new Irish art. Curated by the writer Lucy Lippard, this exhibition visited New York and other American cities. Whether or not people understood this work, I never knew, though the books did receive a lot of attention at the time and I greatly enjoyed making them. However, it was not the kind of work from which I could make a living, so I had to let it go.

By the late 1990s, I was still painting rural landscapes and producing large flower paintings. However, I wanted to paint more about psychological states of mind and so I developed a show on the theme of depression. In her book

Modern Art in Ireland, the art critic Dorothy Walker featured some of my self-portraits, called 'Pain Suffering and Despair', in which I tried to express the uniqueness of personal experiences with depression, feelings that can't really be shared. I also developed work on the theme of homophobia, which combined images from found objects with painting. At the time, galleries were unwilling to show art of this nature, not even work that featured male nudity and male sexuality. Changing attitudes and the Internet soon brought everyone closer to such diversity.

In 2000, a visit to my son Orion, who was working as a chemical engineer in Amsterdam, opened my eyes to a more liberal and free-thinking society, where people were friendly, self-confident and non-judgemental. From then on I began to visit some of the major cities in Europe and elsewhere, although I stopped going to the USA after 9/11. All the propaganda about Islam and terrorism made me want to better understand what was really going on. When I visited Istanbul, I found that there was more to see there than I could ever have imagined. I had a sense of being part of history itself, in a city where all the world could meet. I began visiting the city more and more and, since 2005, Istanbul has been my home. I paint images of life there – the mosques, markets and shrines, local customs like bathing in 600-year-old bathhouses, drinking tea from glass-tulip cups and the like. I have been transported to a new kind of life. Places like Anatolia, Western Turkey and the Mediterranean shores are amazing with their temples and palaces, about which little is really known. Fethiye and Antalya are two cities that stand out because of the light and their closeness to many archaeological wonders, such as the old ruined city of Ephesus, which has only been partly excavated. While living in Turkey, I continue to exhibit back in Ireland.

12

John Keating

*Photograph by
Lar Boland*

I was born in 1953 and raised in Clonmel, County Tipperary, the eldest – and only boy – in a family of four. My father, Pierce Keating, was a second-generation woodturner and furniture and cabinet maker. My mother, Nora Hayes, trained as a chiropodist in London after World War II and was one of the first formally trained chiropodists in Ireland. My parents were childhood sweethearts, who were brought up in Cahir but moved to Clonmel after they married. Both were hugely influential in my life and did everything possible to support my career as an artist. My father was a real craftsman, who loved to design as well as manufacture elaborate staircases, balustrades and the like. As a child, I would spend time in his workshop carving bits of discarded wood and this introduced me to a studio atmosphere.

At primary school in Clonmel, I was taught by Molly Bracken, an amazing woman with interests in music, the arts, gardening, bee-keeping and much, much more. In the days of greater innocence, local children would go to her house after school to paint and sculpt. She encouraged me to enter the Caltex (now the Texaco) Children's Art Competition when I was about 5 or 6 and I won a national prize. I can still recall travelling up to Dublin's Gresham Hotel and being presented with my prize by the then President, Sean T. O'Ceallaigh. I think that Sean Keating, who was then the president of the RHA, was one of the judges. This was a magical experience for somebody so young and probably set me on my future path.

I went to secondary school at Clonmel's High School, run by the Christian Brothers, where there was no emphasis on art. However, from the age of 7 or 8, I regularly attended evening art classes in the local vocational school (the 'Tech'), where, among others, I was taught by Walter Verling and Barry Moloney. As I was finishing secondary school, Barry was appointed principal of the Crawford School of Art in Cork and it was an easy decision for me to follow Barry to the Crawford, from which I obtained a degree in fine arts. I then

Looking North; oil and acrylic on
canvas; 2012; 120 × 100cm.

THE OLD PIER, UNION HALL

spent four years as an art teacher at a new comprehensive school in the village of Boherbue in North Cork. This was an exciting job in a progressive and well-equipped school and I had a free hand in developing the new art department.

I painted throughout this time and exhibited a little in Cork city galleries. However, I was probably not working as I should and might well have stagnated as an artist were it not for a three-month spell in New York during the summer of 1976. While there, I explored the Guggenheim, Metropolitan and other major galleries and was both unsettled and inspired by what I saw. I walked in off the street to a commercial gallery on Madison Avenue, showed them images of my work and was invited to contribute to an upcoming group exhibition, where my work was well received and reviewed. A chance encounter and a random act of kindness put me in contact with the famous Art Students League of New York – the largest independent art college in the world. I was offered a scholarship which allowed me to work there for an academic year in 1980–81, following in the footsteps of such famous artists as Thomas Eakins, Mark Rothko, Roy Lichtenstein, Jackson Pollock and Norman Rockwell.

By then I had met my future wife, Miriam O'Meara, in Dublin. Miriam writes and works in theatre and is an exciting influence in my life. We married in 1981 and our twin daughters, Ruth and Rebecca, were born in 1991. We now live in Dalkey, County Dublin, and I have a studio in the back garden. Though based in Ireland for most of my life, at different times I have worked and exhibited in Barcelona and Monte Carlo. More recently, I have gravitated towards Italy, where I spend a few weeks each year. Nowadays, I am probably as well known in Italy as in Ireland. While I am represented by a gallery in Milan, I also exhibit in the Lake Como and Lake Garda regions, in Turin, Abruzzo, Bergamo, Florence, Genoa and Rome.

I mostly paint in oils and watercolour but also enjoy figurative work in charcoal. Different media have their own temperament, their own intrinsic qualities, which lend themselves to different subject matter. For example, the translucency of light that you get in a Mediterranean garden lends itself to watercolour. In my subject matter, I'm particularly interested in exploring the interplay between the stated and the suggested. By this I mean that, in depicting an object, I strive merely to suggest and allow the observer's imagination to add to the visual experience. By suggesting a bit, you tend to convey more. For this reason, I like to depict fragments. On trips to Greece, I have been greatly taken with bits of broken columns and statues that are strewn around ancient sites. I also see these as metaphors for the human condition, human frailty and vulnerability, of the striving for perfection in life that so often leads to broken stone – disappointment, fragmentation and disintegration.

I mostly work from my studio. I am fairly disciplined and work most days. It generally takes me some time to warm up each day, but, once I'm engaged, I become totally absorbed, to the extent that I lose track of time. Working raises my spirits and I often feel a mood change shortly after I begin. I tend to build up images over time using drawing, props, source material and photographic information. When developing a composition, I tend to experiment with different approaches and reject these one by one until I find one strong element that holds the work together. There was a time when I hated the notion of parting with my work, but I had to 'get real' and accept that I wouldn't be able to continue as an artist if I didn't sell. Miriam retains pieces of work from different periods.

Over the years I have received a number of significant awards and accolades, including two gold medals. The first was for a national survey of painting in Bergamo about ten years ago. More recently, I was chosen to represent Ireland at the 2012 London Olympic Fine Arts event, run in conjunction with the Olympic Games. There, I won a gold medal of honour for a painting, *Oriental Lilies*, which is now held with some of the other exhibited work in Beijing. There have been just two other Irish Olympic medal winners for art – Jack B. Yeats in the 1924 Paris Olympics and Letitia Hamilton in the 1948 London Olympics – and I feel honoured to be in such exalted company. Also in 2012, I won the Art Water Cube Cup Award at an International Painting and Calligraphic Exhibition in Beijing, and I was one of fifty international artists invited to exhibit at the 5th International Biennale 'Stemperando' in Rome in 2013.

I think I will continue to paint for as long as I can move. I never really stop painting. For example, if sitting in a crowded train, I'm likely to be observing my fellow passengers and particularly those of different nationalities, wondering how I might paint them and what colours I'd need to mix to get a particular shade. Essentially, I observe the world as an artist.

13

Carin Mac Cana

encouraging. My grandfather was an avid art collector and our house had a lot of his paintings and sculptures on display. He was Dean at Linkoping's Cathedral and Chairman of the County Arts Society, and was very supportive to a lot of artists. He commissioned a Norwegian artist, Sorensen, to paint the cathedral's altarpiece – these were rather modern pieces for the time. One uncle was an art historian and another an artist. It was his drawings that really first inspired me – I was fascinated by his mark-making, by how a line on a page could become something real. There were also a lot of art books in our house and I would spend hours alone with them, looking and absorbing. The family bible also had great illustrations.

My father worked for the city public transport company and kept getting promoted, so we moved around the country a lot. We never spent more than five years in one place and perhaps this contributed to my own wanderlust. In 1970 he became chief of Uppsala City Bus, so we moved there, having spent the previous five years in Malmö. By this stage, I had become quite rebellious. It was an exciting time of political and social upheaval, so I found Uppsala quite stifling and I couldn't wait to get away and see the world. As soon as I finished school, I went to America and stayed there for a year, working and travelling. I mostly lived in the Dolores Park area of San Francisco, overlooking the city and bay. It was a wonderful time. I modelled for a while for an art

I was born in Sweden and spent my formative years there. My father's family came from the west coast – the area around Gothenburg – and my mother's family from the very north, bordering Finland. As a child I was always drawing and painting. I also had a very vivid imagination, staging my own theatre plays, acting all roles, and doing my own installations, gathering all the interesting and valuable items I could find. My parents were both interested in art and were very

Untitled; acrylic on canvas; 2013;
120 × 100cm.

THE OLD PIER, UNION HALL

class at a university where the professor was a very good teacher and where I got to do some painting.

When I returned home, I couldn't settle and moved to Copenhagen, which was then and still is a very cosmopolitan city. I went to live in Christiania – a sort of experimental 'free town' in an area containing the old city defences and which had stood empty for years until some Danes decided to occupy the empty buildings and build new homes there. By the time I arrived, the place was very established and highly organised through communal meetings. There were restaurants, bars and cafés, a theatre, a bakery, a grocery and hardware shops and a bathhouse, so we had little reason to go into town. In spite of some problems with drugs and criminal elements, it was quite an idyllic place to live. There were no cars, plenty of green space and a river to swim in. And all of this in the middle of a lovely big city! We felt very privileged.

After two years there I decided that I needed some art education and applied to the Arts and Crafts School and to the Royal Academy. To my great surprise, I got a place at the Academy but soon realised that I wasn't ready for this. I was too inexperienced and there wasn't much teaching. Most of the students already had years of art college behind them. We were given huge studios and the professor would visit once a week. I felt a bit lost and, besides, life in Christiania was too distracting. We did, however, have access to the Royal Danish Ballet at the Opera House next door and could draw the dancers as they were practising. This was quite a privilege.

Then, in 1980, I met an Irishman and we had a son, Tristan. My husband whisked me off to Ireland to live in an old Victorian house in West Cork – Lettercollum House. It had served as a convent for many years and, together with a group of family and friends, we bought it to live there as a kind of commune. We worked in the walled gardens, growing our own vegetables and trying to improve the big house. It was very cold and we didn't have much money, but it was a good place for children, with plenty of space to play. Later the place became a hostel, serving very good vegetarian meals, and later still, as the house improved, it evolved into a kind of eccentric guest house, serving famous Sunday lunches. The big house was sold in early 2000 and only two of the original owners still reside there, in the converted stables.

My marriage sadly didn't work out and on our separation I considered moving back to Denmark. However, I had finally realised that what I really wanted to do was art, so I approached the Crawford College in Cork, which looked very exciting. My son was 3 years old by now, so I had to make a decision. I applied and was accepted. I could have gone straight into second year but opted instead to start afresh, in what was then called the foundation year. It was a very stimulating and interesting learning experience – we could try lots of different media and techniques and, unlike now, I had ample work space. I opted for painting as my main study area and glass as a subsidiary. During my second year in college, my father died suddenly. I was badly affected by this and took a year out. I graduated in 1989 with distinction and won Student of the Year. The prize was a solo show at the Cork Arts Society premises on Lavitt's Quay. I sold a lot of work at this, which was very encouraging.

My work at that time was figurative but I didn't really understand then what it was about. Only later did I see it as cathartic and about my own life. I continued working like that for a while then tired of it and started undoing the figure, breaking up the surface and moving the figure in and out of the picture plane, abstracting it. This led me to look at the visual elements more and at the composition, simplifying things and being concerned only with form, colour and space. It felt liberating, but it was also difficult to prevent the work from becoming just decorative.

In 1995 I met a Belgian man and some years later we went to Cuba for a month's holiday. When we returned to Ireland I did a series of work based on our time there. The paintings were abstract but had many bits of Cuban nature and culture in them. We married in 2011 and now live on the Sheep's Head peninsula, near Bantry. I teach art part-time and the rest of the time I paint. I look to nature and biology for visual inspiration, but, although some of my work is based on elements of the material world, I don't intend for it to be representative of reality in any way. The forms are deliberately distorted and are not symbolic, at least not consciously. I seek to create a pictorial dynamic that contains both tension and balance between forms and has spatial movement through colour interaction, without falling prey to pattern and decoration.

The arrangement of shapes is spontaneous and intuitive: an initial and very quick drawing, using charcoal and diluted paint, in direct response to the shape and size of the canvas. The colour areas are not planned – I simply apply and see what happens, saturating and building up layer after layer, sometimes changing the colour or the tone. I strive for ambiguity in form and space, and movement in colour and light.

14

Michael McCarthy

I was born in Mallow, County Cork, in 1942 but grew up in various parts of the world. My father, Michael (Mac) McCarthy, joined the RAF during World War II and was sent to Malaya shortly afterwards. During this time, my younger brother was born and was nearly three years old when my father returned home in 1949. My father was a talented amateur artist but the war years restricted his creativity. My mother, Mary (Queenie) Egan, came originally from Tralee. There were six children in her family. In 1950, my father was posted to Coastal Command at Aldergrove, near Belfast, and the family moved there with him. Still later, we all spent time in Baghdad before moving to Newark-on-Trent, an old Roman town near Nottingham in England. My father then left the services, with little or no pension, and money was scarce. From an early age, this gave me a sense of discipline and an understanding of the need for hard work.

My schooling was quite fragmented due to all the family moves. My first experiments in art as a small child were drawing on biscuit tins in school and doing sand drawings. When we moved to Northern Ireland, I went from a 700-pupil school to one with just 28 pupils in three classes, which meant that I benefited from a great deal of individual attention, including art tuition. My schooling in Baghdad was equally wonderful, with about 80 students, first-class facilities and all the art materials that one could hope for. At the time, there were quite a number of art students on national service in Iraq and they were always keen to teach the children of other servicemen. I acquired my first sketchbook in Iraq and remember sketching the wonderful eucalyptus trees on the banks of the Euphrates River. My school in Newark was new, progressive and well-resourced, with highly motivated teaching staff. The few Roman Catholics, Jews and other minorities were excused religious education and, instead, I had double the exposure to art. I left school at 15 and went directly to art college, where I spent two years under the tutelage of the noted English artist Robert Kiddey. There, I studied life drawing, painting and pictorial composition.

Summer Morning Stillness, Union Hall; oil on canvas; 2010; 37 × 75cm.

On leaving art college, I found it impossible to find a placement in a commercial studio, as the British economy was in such poor shape. I tried to make a modest living freelancing but simply didn't have the wherewithal for this, so, at the age of 19 I followed my father's advice and joined the RAF. By then, I had become a keen and successful amateur boxer and the RAF not only provided me with the facilities to keep in good physical shape but also to further my artistic studies. I was posted to Cyprus and based near the beautiful Kyrenia Harbour in the island's north. It was a painter's paradise. On returning to the UK, I was posted to the Air Ministry in Whitehall, just a short walk from the National Art Gallery, where I spent many a happy lunch hour studying such greats as Constable, Turner and the French Impressionists.

My long-term plan was to emigrate to Australia, so in 1966 I took the '£10 assisted passage' to Sydney. I got a job in the coastal town of Nowra, 100 miles south of Sydney on the Shoalhaven River. The surrounding coastline and inland scenery were just magnificent and one of the first things I did there was to buy myself a box of paints. I found that I was living in the same street in Nowra as the revered Australian landscape painter Leonard Long. He soon took me under his wing and encouraged me to become a landscape painter. We would often 'go bush' together on painting expeditions. Leonard was 100 years old in 2011 and painted right up to then, culminating in a centenary show of his life's work and travels.

Family circumstances then obliged me to return to England for a while, but I was eventually able to make my way back to New South Wales in 1972. I quickly teamed up again with Leonard Long and with another colleague, John Downton. With local commissions, I was able to survive and to keep painting outdoors. My first Sydney exhibition, opened by Leonard, was a complete success and this was the beginning of my life as a professional artist.

For me, the greatest joy is in painting *en plein air*. However, after twenty years of travelling around Australia, sometimes working in temperatures of 95–100 degrees, there was a price to pay and I eventually found a small 'bump' on my shoulder which turned out to be a malignant melanoma. My surgeon told me that if I had ignored it, I would have been in serious trouble within six months. Thank heavens I've had no recurrence of it since. When I see people jumping up and down because they've won a few million in the lottery, I have a quiet little smile to myself and say another prayer in gratitude. Thank God for modern medicine and the health professionals who mind us!

After I began to paint full-time, I settled into a routine of rising early and getting out to paint in the early morning light. Leaving home with two blank canvases and returning in the evening with two completed works is probably as great an experience as you are likely to have in life. It's great for the mind, the heart and the soul. I produced enough work for two or three exhibitions a year and I well remember bringing my mother to Sydney after my father died and dedicating an exhibition to them at a wonderful gallery in Windsor, New South Wales, on the Hawkesbury River. I was then approached by a hotelier who was planning to build an Irish-themed hotel and wanted to include some original Irish paintings. He sponsored me to spend six weeks in Ireland, during which time I produced 45 small paintings. I travelled through the strife-torn north to the Mourne Mountains and to the Antrim coast and then on to Connemara, Kerry, Cork, Waterford, Wexford and Wicklow, mostly painting from the side of the road. For a number of years thereafter, I held a number of sell-out shows in Sydney and Brisbane that featured my paintings of Irish scenes.

In 1992, I was invited to spend a year as Artist in Residence at the Institute of Forest Genetics at Placerville, in the foothills of the Sierra Nevada Mountains in California. Being based in such a fabulous setting and having my work respected by some of the leading scientists in their fields was both an amazing and life-changing experience for me. On returning to Australia, I was invited to exhibit some landscapes of Ireland at an exhibition to commemorate the 150th anniversary of the Irish Famine at the famous town of Yass. By now, I had met and married my Australian wife, Helen, and in 1997 we decided to work in Ireland for a year and to have some European adventures. Friends rented us their home at Lanesborough on the Shannon and we quickly established ourselves with some good Irish galleries. I was soon invited to participate in the Irish Millennium Tour in Belfast and Dublin with artists from Spain, Russia, Israel and the UK, together with the Irish artist Norman McCaig.

Somehow or other, our intention back in 1997 of spending a year in Ireland has stretched to sixteen years and we are now well settled in Killashee in County Longford. My work is available through several commercial galleries throughout Ireland and has made its way to Government House in Sydney, Leinster House in Dublin, the University of California and to public collections in places as far apart as Holland and Peru. I've been very fortunate in my career.

15

Avril McDermott

was never going to be mine, so I left second-level education at the age of 15, which in the 1970s was not at all unusual. I then furthered my education at a secretarial college, which I left with my shorthand typing certificate. My first job as a secretary earned me the vast sum of £10 per week at the age of 16.

I was married quite young and unfortunately my marriage didn't last. I sold the family home in Dublin and moved to County Westmeath with my five children: Gary, Jenny, Stuart, Graham and Daniel. Sadly, Daniel died in 2004; he had severe cerebral palsy. Life was not easy for my children, but they have all done well in life. Gary now works as a highly respected graphic designer in Paris, Jenny works in the equestrian industry, Stuart is an accountant and Graham is studying the culinary arts in Galway. I also have a grand-daughter called Murryn. We're a pretty close-knit family and, despite the fact that they didn't grow up here, I like to think that my place in Union Hall now serves as a second home for my children and grandchild. I also love to visit my kids. For example, I manage to visit Gary in Paris every now and again and even manage to get some ideas for paintings while there.

From as far back as I can remember, I have wanted to paint and can clearly recall painting murals on my bedroom walls as a child. Years later, as a young, single mother and with very little money, I used to make my painting surfaces by spreading polyfilla on hardboard and painting

I was brought up in a kind and loving home in Clontarf, Dublin, but have strong connections with West Cork. My father, John McDermott, was a building contractor and my mother, Eileen, helped to run the family business. My elder brother and only sibling, Mervyn, worked with my father until his death at the age of 37 following an accident. I had a comfortable upbringing, first attending Greenlanes National School in Clontarf and then Bertrand & Rutland High School in the centre of Dublin city. However, a life of academia

Untitled; oil on canvas; 2013; 48 × 57.5cm.

wallpaper paste over that. It actually made a very good platform to work on, so with my two paintbrushes and my primary colours I used to set to work as soon as the children were in bed. I would paint until the early hours of the morning. I hadn't a clue about what I was doing, but I was determined to learn and that I did. I kept painting and looking at the technique of other artists, asking questions all the time. I became obsessive and would paint every day, all of the time trying to teach myself. I particularly threw myself into my art after Daniel's death and this helped me to cope with my enormous loss.

I then started to show my work. When you step into that arena, you look at the work of other artists and realise that, no matter how good you feel your own work to be, there is always someone better. The lesson to be learnt is that you have to keep raising your game in order to become the very best that you can possibly be. I have served my time hanging my work on the railings in St Stephen's Green – the People's Art. Now that's dedication – hail, rain or snow, you're out in it or in Merrion Square every Sunday, all year round. I did that for years, maybe selling nothing or something, but I never stopped trying. For years I was a participant every August at the RDS during Horse Show week and in the Art Ireland exhibition, also at the RDS, in November. These were all positive experiences and proved to be a great learning curve. All of the artists that I have come to know over the years have brought something to me and to my work. We are normally a generous lot and we don't mind sharing.

I moved to West Cork in 2011, my family being then independent of me. I spent about two and a half years looking for a house and searched all over West Cork. I very nearly bought a place a couple of times, but, for various reasons, all of the deals fell through at the last minute. Then I found out about a house for sale in Union Hall. I well remember my first visit to the village and thinking how beautiful the place was. I fell for the house as soon as I saw it and the sale went through with no hassle within a few weeks. Looking back on it, I think that my Union Hall home was waiting for me and this might well explain why the other transactions fell through. Some things are just meant to be. West Cork in general, and Union Hall in particular, is an artist's paradise. Although I am new to village life, having spent over twenty years in rural and often remote places, I really enjoy the bustle of village life and have good neighbours. Also, the people in West Cork definitely have an appreciation of the arts.

I find it difficult to clearly express my approach to painting. I mostly paint indoors and am not the type of artist who toddles around with an easel in the great outdoors. I use photography a lot to help me capture an image. I don't draw or sketch. Rather, I start with a basic shape and use brushwork to create an image. Over the years, my development as an artist has caused me to look at things in a different way. I love equestrian subjects, though there's not a huge demand for this in West Cork. I also love to paint village scenes, landscapes and seascapes. The media that I use are oils and watercolours, but I am also going to try my hand at pastels in the near future. Like many artists, I am fascinated by the constantly changing light in West Cork. It really is the most fantastic place for any artist to live and work.

There is a scene to be painted around every corner. I paint at my home in Union Hall and have a workshop where I do my own framing. For me, the environment in which I paint is not important, as I could paint anywhere.

The year 2013 has been a pretty momentous one for me, as this was the year in which I published my book *Time and Place*. The book is based around a series of oil paintings of the iconic villages of West Cork – 29 in total. The idea behind this came from my son Gary, who suggested producing a calendar of such paintings. Instead, I decided to publish a book with images of all 29 paintings, together with a complimentary piece of local history on each of the villages. My good friend Ann O'Connor from Leap did a fantastic job researching and writing about each of the villages. My original plan was to keep the collection together and have it tour various venues in West Cork. However, since the book launch, I've been approached by people who wanted to buy individual paintings and I've reluctantly had to let them go. This project was hugely enjoyable to start with, but, to be honest, it started to become a bit tedious towards the end, particularly with a deadline looming for publication, and I was glad when the project finally came to an end. The book launch in July succeeded beyond my wildest dreams and I was so very grateful to the people of the village who came out to support me in their droves.

I'm now at work on my next project but don't really want to say too much about this until I'm more confident about the direction it is taking. My life as an artist is never boring. I absolutely adore what I do, which is why I do it every day of my life and will continue on for as long as I draw breath.

16

Arthur Maderson

I was born in Clapham, south London, on 27 December 1942, the middle child in a family of three. I was christened Arthur Karl. Sadly, my parents were trapped in a destructive and dysfunctional relationship, turning to the bottle in a futile attempt to escape and find solace from a profoundly unhappy marriage. My only refuge was my grandmother, Flo, who lived upstairs in the same house and who steadfastly provided support, comfort and love at a critical stage in my development. Through the war I was evacuated for short periods to Corby, Northamptonshire. However, I spent most of the war years in London and was there during much of the heaviest bombing. My home suffered a number of near misses, including from a V2 rocket that devastated a series of houses in our street.

At a very early age – 6 or 7 – I let it be known that I wanted to be a painter. A number of photos from this period survive showing me painting at an easel. With no immediate connection with art in my family, there exists a genetic link with a Victorian Scottish Academician on my mother's side. In 1959, at the age of 17, I went to the Camberwell School of Art in Peckham in south-east London, where I studied fine art for four years. My father mistakenly believed that I was studying commercial art and wouldn't have approved of me trying to make a career in fine art. I was almost qualified by the time he learned the truth. While Camberwell was not in the forefront of avant-garde art schools, it placed emphasis on solid, traditional techniques and skills. Robert Medley was head of the college, which included amongst its teaching staff such internationally renowned artists as Frank Auerbach, Ron Kitaj and Patrick Procktor.

THE OLD PIER, UNION HALL

After art college, an earlier interest in psychology and psychiatry led me in the direction of exploring the possibilities of using art as a developmental tool in the process of rehabilitation in both penal and mental institutions. In 1970 I accepted the post of Head Art Therapist at Park Prewett Hospital, Basingstoke, Hampshire, a position which I held for eight years. I then moved to Street in Somerset and worked as a clinical tutor at the British Institute for Brain Injured Children at Knowle Hall, Bridgwater. Here, my responsibilities included the organisation and reassessment of individual programmes of physical and neurological developmental activities for brain-injured children. I became an experienced freelance lecturer in further education and have held classes in Hampshire and Somerset, where I also taught painting and chess. My essential fascination is with the (not as yet fully understood) physiological and psychological mechanisms of perception. Although I enjoyed the challenge and stimulus of this work, in 1980 I decided to devote all of my energies to painting full-time.

It was not until 1982 that I began to exhibit my paintings. Few examples of my work prior to this have survived, as I destroyed the major part of my output. My progress, and indeed my success as a professional painter, in this period was rapid. In many ways I have been oblivious to current fads and trends in painting. Instead, I pursue my own goal, which is to fully integrate the image into the picture surface with a fierce determination, fully convinced that the organisational demands of the picture itself do not contradict the subtle exploration of the rich kaleidoscope of 'raw' visual information. By 'raw' information I mean information that is uncontaminated by preconceived ideas as to what it should look like, the final pictorial statement being the outcome of this struggle. I constantly need to trust in what is actually seen, as opposed to seeing what is believed to exist. This 'raw' information is infinitely surprising and varied and capable of numerous levels of interpretation. Concepts of local colour disappear, and I allow forms, whether in landscape or figure study, to emerge or evaporate as they do in nature. It is light we primarily see, and conclusions as to what this light in fact 'represents' are a secondary matter, to be relished as a joint enterprise with the spectator, who is compelled to participate in the process of exploring possibilities of interpretation. In an article in the *Artist* magazine, I described the process as follows:

> Whilst we have an intellectual understanding of the separateness of the objects, they arrive on our retina in a fully integrated and delightful state of chaos. To resort to illustration in order to give the spectator an easy ride is to insult their visual intelligence – an intelligence which actually thrives on the mysterious process of scanning a wide range of possibilities. For me the pictures are fuel for the imagination. The spectator's role is changing rapidly, no longer the detached observer of other people's skills, but rather as a very active participant.

In 1987 I moved from Somerset to a totally isolated 17th-century Welsh longhouse high in the Cambrian Mountains, without electricity or a

January, Towards Sunset, Keelbeg, Near Union Hall; oil on panel; 2013; 118 × 118cm.

phone. This move, against my agent's advice to 'move to London', indicated both a single-minded aspect of my personality combined with a reclusive tendency. I do not court publicity or move in 'artistic circles', nor do I have a website and I am almost impossible to contact by phone. My wife Verlayne and I moved to Cappoquin in County Waterford in 1989, when I was in my late 40s. We have three children, Ciara, Jess and Padraig. Ciara is training as a psychiatric nurse, Jess is a musician and teaches cello, while Padraig is also a musician. I also have two children, Ben and Sam, from a previous marriage. Ben is a chef and does all of my framing, while Sam is a stonemason.

I had established a formidable reputation in the UK by the time I moved to Cappoquin. A move to relative obscurity in Ireland meant that I had to start building a reputation all over again. However, I have since become recognised as one of Ireland's strongest figurative painters. My first one-man show in Dublin proved to be a stunning success; in fact, all of my one-man exhibitions in the Republic have sold out. I have exhibited at the Royal Academy of London and have been an award winner at the West of England Academy and at the Royal Hibernian Academy.

Whilst I continue to paint on a regular basis, I rarely exhibit my work. I now paint primarily for pleasure and have been reluctant to sell my recent work, which I put aside for the eventual benefit of my family. My working life is now shared between the Blackwater Valley in County Waterford and the mountainous Cévennes region in the south of France. The few people who know me well realise that I am genuinely surprised by and grateful for my artistic success.

17

Meadhbh O'Donoghue

I was born in 1995 and have lived in the Cork suburb of Bishopstown for all my life to date. My Dad, Patrick O'Donoghue (who everybody calls 'Pod'), is an entrepreneur. My Mom, Deirdre McKeon, is a nurse-midwife. Both have been a huge influence in my life and I'm not just saying that. I have three brothers. The eldest, Eoin, is a real high-flyer, with an Honours degree in Construction Management and a Masters in Town Planning, despite the fact that he's been profoundly deaf since birth. Eoin now lives in London. He also plays soccer for the Irish Deaf Team and has something like 35 Irish caps. He's amazing! The next oldest, Larry, is also a high-flyer. He recently qualified as a pilot with Aer Lingus and is now based in Dublin. I spend the most time with my last brother, Patrick, who is two years younger than me. We also have a dog called Benson, who is a Labradoodle and is a big part of all our lives.

I went to primary school at Gaelscoil Uí Riada near my home in Bishopstown. I really loved it there and, as everything was done through Irish, I'm fluent in and love the language. I first started to draw, colour and paint at the Gaelscoil – this is really where it all started for me. To begin with, the art classes were mostly around Christmas and other seasonal stuff, but, as we got older, we were encouraged to become more adventurous. My Dad has kept a folder of a lot of the work that I produced at the Gaelscoil. I then went to secondary school at Coláiste Choilm in Ballincollig, where there were three art teachers, two of whom – Niamh O'Neill and Áine Andrews – taught me. Both are also professional artists. I had most contact with Ms O'Neill and loved being part of her art classes. She paints in an impressionistic style and I find that this interests me more and more. I am now studying for my Leaving Certificate at Bruce College at the top of Patrick's Hill in Cork city. Here, I have three hours of art education weekly – two hours of practical work and one of art theory. Art theory includes

The Pier at Night; acrylic on canvas; 2013; 46 × 60cm.

visits to local galleries and we were recently brought to see Robert Ballagh's 'Seven' exhibition at the Crawford Gallery. This was just fantastic; I particularly liked his portrait of the singer Eleanor McEvoy.

I did my first painting on Christmas Day 1998 when I was 3 years and 20 days old. Mum had it framed and it still hangs in my Dad's office. I'd draw or paint every day if I had the time. Once I start, I can spend the whole day painting. When I start something, I try to finish it on the same day, otherwise it might never get finished. My preference is for painting outdoors and I like to work with what's in front of me, to see it from different angles and in this way to get a feel for the subject. I tend not to work from photographs, as I find it limiting to work in just two dimensions. When drawing, I like to sketch people, but, when painting, I prefer landscapes. I have drawn portraits of famous people like Jessie J and Ellie Goulding – my two favourite singers. However, I don't think that either of these drawings is much good. I haven't yet done any drawings of my family. I sketch in pencil, ink and charcoal and I paint in acrylics. I haven't yet tried painting in oils but hope to do so soon. Greens and blues are my favourite colours.

My Mum's sister, Auntie Aileen, lives in Union Hall and I've been visiting there since before I was born, so I know the place really well. When I visit, I like to spend time on the beach beside the old pier with Benson (my dog). I also love to walk in Rineen Woods and to see if any new fairy houses have been built since my last visit. The painting of the old pier that I've produced for this book was commissioned by my Dad. He paid me €100 for it, which is pretty cool, particularly as it's my very first commission. It's based on a night-time photo taken by my Dad. The pier at Union Hall is very brightly lit at night, presumably because the fishing boats come and go at all hours. I found it very hard to capture the effect of light and was only able to do so by building up layer after layer of white paint. The background was much easier to paint and I loved doing that part. I got most of the painting done on the first day but then put it aside for a while, so that, in all, I worked on it for about three months. I'm not sure if it's much good and I'm not really all that pleased with it, but it's the best that I can do for now.

Until now, I've liked my paintings to be as precise and as close to real life as possible. However, I'm coming around to liking impressionistic work, especially since studying the work of the Impressionists at school. I particularly like the work of Claude Monet and his use of colour. We watched a movie about his life and work at school and this was really interesting – the way he could paint a picture in a few minutes and could capture the light at a certain time of day. He mostly painted outdoors and this is not an easy thing to do. My favourite Irish artist is Arthur Maderson, who is also an impressionist painter. We have a fantastic painting by him at home. My Mom delivered one of his children a few years ago and she got to know him at that time. When I get the chance, I like to visit art galleries and from time to time go to art auctions with my folks. Art auctions are great in that they allow you to see a wide variety of work. The Crawford Art Gallery in Cork is one of my favourite places. I particularly like the sculptures there.

I'm definitely going to paint in my future life even if I don't manage to make a career from art. I stopped painting for a while a few years ago, dropped art as a subject at school and took up chemistry instead. I soon realised that this was a big mistake and so I went back to art. I really missed it so much. I've been warned by my Dad and others that being an artist can be a tough life. You can put your heart and soul into a painting and then find that nobody likes it enough to want to buy it. You can spend a lot of time on things that might not be rewarding. I hope to be one of the few who succeed in making a career of it. I think that I'd enjoy teaching art as well and maybe I could make a living from this. Anyway, I hope to go to art college either in Cork (the Crawford), Dublin or Limerick when I finish secondary school and am now starting to put together a portfolio for this.

Apart from art, animals are my other great love. I've been horse-riding since the age of 4 or 5 but had to stop this recently as my back started to hurt and I found that I had a disc out of place – whatever that is. This wasn't from a fall or anything. I've only ever fallen from a horse about three times and never really hurt myself when I fell. I mostly did cross-country and didn't ever do much jumping. Another problem is that I'm allergic to most animals, including horses. I would get hay fever, runny eyes and constant colds when I used to ride regularly.

If I couldn't be an artist, I have no real idea what I'd like to be. I might work in business like my Dad or do something creative, like be an interior designer or something. I once thought I'd like to be a vet, but my allergies to dogs, cats and horses might be a problem. Also, I think that I might get too attached to the animals in my care. Being a doctor might be OK, as I like helping people. I once spent a week in hospital on work experience and found this very interesting. However, more than anything, I want to be an artist.

18

Diāna Pivovarova

I'm originally from Latvia and was brought up in Jēkabpils, a town of about 30,000 people some 140km southeast of Riga. I went to both primary and secondary school there and, from the age of 8, also studied piano at the local School of Music. I had just one sibling – my sister Larisa –

who is seven years older than me. Though my father died suddenly from a stroke at the age of 38, when I was just 6 years old, he was a big influence on my life. He was a policeman and had a great interest in art, read widely on the subject and painted a little. One of my earliest memories is the smell of my father's oil paints and, to this day, the smell of paint reminds me of my father. He also collected a huge number of art books and magazines and I began to read these in my teens. I still have some of my father's art books, which are among my most treasured possessions. My mother was also a very positive influence in my life and encouraged me in every possible way.

For me, music and painting are totally entwined and are just different forms of artistic expression. Initially, music was my main focus and, by the age of 13, I had decided to become a professional musician. After secondary school and having also graduated from the Jēkabpils Music School at the age of 17, I studied piano for four years at the College of Music in Rezekne. I was a talented pianist and had a particular passion for the music of Bach. I met and married my husband, Val, while I was still at college and I was aged just 20 when our daughter Alex was born. After graduation, the College of Music offered me a teaching position and so I spent another year at Rezekne. By then, Val had gone to work in construction in Western Siberia in Russia and I followed him there in 1982, also working in construction. This was a very remote and male-

Untitled; oil on canvas; 2009; 30 × 100cm.

dominated environment, but life there had its romantic aspects. I did the same work as the men, even working with compressors and other heavy machinery. Val and I later moved to the Chinese border in Eastern Siberia and there I got a teaching job in the local school of music.

Much as I have loved music, there are aspects that I find frustrating. Firstly, it is highly demanding, obliging me to practise for four or five hours each day. Secondly, after finishing a recital, a musician has little that's tangible to show for her efforts – the music pretty much disappears into the air. Through my 20s and 30s I drew a little, but not in a serious way. However, I did a lot of craftwork as a hobby, for example making leather handbags and upholstering domestic furniture in leather. In 1999, when aged in my early 40s, I returned to Jēkabpils and enrolled in a course in interior design at the local art school. I took up painting quite suddenly and took to this like a duck to water. Looking back, I now realise that I had spent my life until then preparing to be a painter. I experienced two life-transforming events at this time, which probably forced this life change. The first was major illness, when I developed encephalitis following a tick bite and became so ill that I was not expected to live. Shortly thereafter, I again narrowly escaped death in a house fire. I realised that life was too short and uncertain not to focus on what was most important and, for me, this was painting.

Of course, I had had an interest in painting all along and this had been stimulated by memories of my father and by some schoolteachers. I took to painting with a degree of enthusiasm that bordered on the obsessive. I would paint until three in the morning and couldn't rise early enough in the morning so that I could get back to work. I initially painted on silk but quickly moved to oil painting. I had my first exhibition just four months after I started painting – a group exhibition with some artistic friends – at which I showed seven works. While these weren't very good, they were better than I could have expected. I then worked with an artist friend and mentor to build up a portfolio of work so that, after two years, I was accepted into the prestigious Latvian Academy of Art in Riga, initially taking painting courses and later enrolling in a BA programme, from which I graduated in 2007 when in my early 50s.

I moved to Ireland immediately after finishing art college. By then, Val had been working in Ireland for five years and I had visited him here about three times a year. We first lived near Athenry in County Galway but later moved to our present home, between Headford and Cong on the Galway–Mayo border. I regard Cong as my home village and my favourite pastime is walking in the woods around Ashford Castle between Lough Corrib and Lough Mask. While I regard these as my own private woods, I love sharing them with others and can never resist bringing visitors for a walk in 'my' woods.

I paint exclusively in oil. It is such a wonderful substance; you can mix any colour that you want. I don't use watercolour and am suspicious of acrylic paint. It's a new medium and, unlike oil painting, nobody knows what an acrylic painting will look like in a hundred years. It also reminds me too much of plastic. I am very diverse in my subject matter. I like to paint landscapes (forests in particular), townscapes, cityscapes, portraits and life drawings. I like to combine my interest in art and music and normally paint with music in the background. I drift with the music and this allows me to paint from my deep subconscious, often using expressive gestures at the expense of an accurate rendition of the subject matter. I have produced a large body of work on music-related themes and these were the focus of a solo exhibition in Dublin in 2008. The colours that I use are also an intuitive response to my mood at any given time and my work hopefully projects the lyrical and poetic source from which it springs.

I'm a restless painter and regularly move between subject matter, even within the same studio session. I paint in all sizes and shapes, though my painting technique varies greatly with the size of canvas. I work *en plein air* and also use photography as a guide. However, most of all, I like to paint from my imagination and to take liberties with the subject matter. This doesn't always please potential buyers, who may ask, for example, about the whereabouts of such and such an imaginary house or why something is not represented in its 'true' colour. I often paint for my own sake, producing a form of work and a palette that I know will have limited appeal to others. Over the years, I've been involved in many group and solo exhibitions in Latvia, Lithuania and Germany, as well as in many parts of Ireland. I have had a particular association with the Morris Gallery in Skibbereen and with the Cong Art Gallery in County Mayo.

I'm at my happiest when I'm painting. I can forget everything else and feel totally free – what it must be like for a bird in flight. A sense of obsession about my work never leaves me – I want to paint, I want to paint, I want to paint.

19

Una Sealy ARHA

Comprehensive at a time when Feedback (later The Hype, then U2) were the school band. I've drawn for as long as I can remember – on school books, exam papers, everything – so that, from quite early on, it was apparent that I would be an artist.

On finishing secondary school in the late 1970s, I went to Dún Laoghaire College of Art & Design – now the Institute of Art, Design & Technology. This was a great experience. At the time, an earlier revolution at the National College of Art and Design (NCAD) had caused some people to decamp to Dún Laoghaire, where they established an outpost of creativity. There was a strong spirit of camaraderie among students and faculty alike and the school felt liberated through being something of an underdog and different to the NCAD. We had some brilliant teachers – the likes of Charlie Tyrrell, Alice Hanratty and Gene Lambert – and a charismatic principal in Trevor Scott. I had a particular regard for the inspirational Donal O'Sullivan, who taught life drawing, an important part of the programme at Dún Laoghaire. Donal died tragically at a young age and, because his work was never really fashionable, he has been largely forgotten. He enjoyed iconic status with those lucky enough to know him at Dún Laoghaire.

While my four years at Dún Laoghaire honed my artistic skills, art college didn't really prepare me for running an art practice. My time of graduation in the early 1980s also coincided with

I was brought up in Howth, a fishing village in north County Dublin, in the 1960s and '70s, the second eldest in a family of four. My parents, Douglas and Mary, were both schoolteachers. I went to school at Sutton Park in Howth, where my father taught me Irish. After Inter Cert, I moved to Mount Temple

THE OLD PIER, UNION HALL

a major economic recession, so that, like many another, I spent several years making a living as best I could. I did sign-writing, painted stage sets, designed restaurant menus and did waitressing – anything that I could get my hands on to support the painting. It was pretty much impossible to sell anything at this time. In 1982 I got the chance to set up a studio with my college friend Phelim Connolly, in an old building on Eustace Street in Dublin's Temple Bar. The building had been acquired by CIE, which was buying up property in the area to demolish in order to build a bus depot. We had a room each on the top floor, had no electricity to start with and had to contend with a leaking roof and freezing cold, but it was a kick-start to our careers. Two other artists later moved in downstairs, an artistic community began to spring up around the area and a campaign developed to establish a cultural quarter in Temple Bar. The rest is now history. We were there at the very beginning, when there was a palpable sense of opportunity and creativity in the air. Those were exciting days.

The year 1985 found me living in a flat in Northumberland Road and still struggling to make a living. In an attempt to take greater control of my life, I applied for a job at the Grapevine Arts Centre (later the City Arts Centre), which was then located in North Frederick Street. I worked there for six years, with its founder and director Sandy Fitzgerald, first helping with its relocation to Moss Street and later ending up as its manager. I helped run the centre's gallery, theatre and café and also became involved with the annual Dublin Street Carnival and with numerous other community arts events. I continued to paint throughout this time. By 1991, I'd come to realise that I'd had enough of administration and was keen to strike out on my own. I held my first solo exhibition at the City Arts Centre in November 1991. This was well received critically and was also a commercial success. Following an invitation to lecture at my old alma mater in Dún Laoghaire, I decided to take a risk, jump ship and try to make my living as an independent artist. For the next five years, I taught painting at Dún Laoghaire two days a week while continuing to paint and to exhibit.

The next major milestone in my life happened in 1996, when I went to San Francisco for the summer to join my partner Chris, forgot to come home and ended up living there for a couple of years. I had a studio in a massive warehouse that my friend, the Cork-born artist Edain O'Donnell, and a couple of others had converted into loft-style living spaces and studios. It was in the Mission district, a mostly Mexican area where accommodation was relatively cheap. I relished the alternative lifestyle, painted full-time, attended life-drawing classes, showed in group exhibitions and gave birth to our first child, Douglas. I blame Chris for hauling me back to Ireland; I would have been quite happy to stay on in San Francisco, at least for a while longer. Once back home, in 1998, I exhibited my San Francisco paintings at Castlebar's Linenhall Arts Centre and later had a solo show in the RHA's Ashford Gallery. More by accident than by design, we all ended up back in Howth, near to where I was brought up, and would now find it hard to move anywhere else. Our second child, Eileen, was born in 2000. Along the way, we acquired two cats and various goldfish, rabbits and gerbils, and I built a studio

Down to the Old Pier, End of Winter; oil on canvas; 2013; 100 × 100cm.

at the bottom of the garden. I continue to teach on workshops in the RHA (where I help to co-ordinate the Schools programme), as well as being an invited tutor on courses in the National Gallery and various third-level colleges.

With regards to my work, the human figure has always been central. While I paint everything from portraits to streetscapes and landscapes, I like to include something of the mark that humans have made on things. Thus a landscape painting might include a shed, a telegraph pole or even a satellite dish. With portraits, I tend to surround my sitters with props and, when painting interiors, I try to find a way to include something of the exterior as well. While I am a great admirer, and will always be in awe of, Velasquez and Rembrandt, I have also been influenced by the 'Kitchen Sink' painters who worked in London in the 1950s, and particularly by the work of John Bratby. Other enduring influences are Bonnard, Édouard Vuillard, Stanley Spencer, Paula Rego, Lucian Freud and Antonio López García.

I paint mostly in oils, occasionally in acrylics and almost always from life. I suppose I don't ever really take a break from painting, as, when I'm not physically doing it, I'm at least thinking about it. To me, everything that I see is a potential painting. I can't imagine a life without painting. That stated, it's a difficult enough life, with lots of hard times financially, and – would I encourage my kids to be professional artists? I'm not sure.

I've had my share of accolades throughout my career to date. Being elected an Associate Member of the RHA in 2010 was an obvious highlight. I've also had a number of Arts Council bursaries and these have helped my professional development and allowed me to travel. My work is in several important collections and I've been selected for group shows in San Francisco, New York and the UK, as well as in Ireland. My painting *Neighbours* won the Ireland–US Council/Irish Arts Review Award for Outstanding Portraiture at the RHA in 2011. I've had eight solo shows, the most recent being a major exhibition in Draíocht Arts Centre in Blanchardstown in late 2012/early 2013. Anyway, back to work . . .

20

Teresa Shanahan

I was brought up on the family farm in the parish of Tracton, near to the sea entrance to Cork Harbour – we could see the beam of the Daunt Lightship from our kitchen. My parents, Joseph Kingston and Margaret (Peggy) Good, to whom we owe eternal gratitude, raised seven children on a 50-acre holding. Farm life exposed me to the cycle of life and seasonal changes, and I clearly recall the impulse to capture something of the joy, life and soul of the ordinary beauty that was part of my country childhood. That sense of innocent delight that comes from feeling close to nature has stayed with me and from those early memories I draw continuous inspiration for my paintings.

I first went to the local national school and then to Scoil na nÓg in Glanmire, County Cork, where I studied through Irish. I was the second in the family and it must have been a relief to our family finances when I won a scholarship to boarding school at Scoil Mhuire, Carrick-on-Suir, County Tipperary. Anseo, d'fhoghlaim mé freisin trí mheán na Gaeilge – I also learnt through Irish there. This was something of a challenge, in that textbooks in Irish were scarce and there were no photocopiers. We were often obliged to copy the teachers' translations of English texts in our own handwriting. Tedious as this was, it did encourage us to develop specific parts of our brains and I think that this later stood me in good stead in my artwork. The arts (literary, dramatic, musical and visual) were held in high esteem in Carrick; there I learned general musicianship, music appreciation and to play the piano. Art was an examination subject and the school had two excellent art teachers. An abiding memory is the half-mile Saturday morning walk along the banks of the River Suir to spend three hours in the school's art studio/loft.

After secondary school, I went to teacher training college at Mary Immaculate in Limerick. In the early 1970s, 'Mary I' had the attributes of a

Untitled; watercolour and gouache on cold-pressed paper; 2013; 35.5 × 56cm.

convent secondary school, but I enjoyed my time there nevertheless. I had the great good fortune to be taught art by the inspirational Walter Verling, who fostered a 'hands-on' approach while also teaching art theory and art appreciation. He made art come alive and made it possible to see pieces through his eyes. He emphasised the power of imagination – 'the window to look out on alternative possibility'. After graduation, I worked at Scoil an Spioraid Naoimh in Bishopstown, Cork – a large city school with over twenty teachers. Then I met my future husband, Denis, and in 1976 – the year we married – I transferred to the two-teacher school in Dreeny Bridge, a few miles from Skibbereen. I loved working there, as it reminded me of the small rural school that I had myself attended as a child. However, when a position nearer home became available I transferred to St Joseph's School in Skibbereen, where I eventually became Deputy-Principal. I retired from St Joseph's in 2010 so that I could devote more time to art. Denis and I have three sons – Colm (b. 1977), Fergus (b. 1979) and Diarmuid (b. 1983), who are all still living and working in Ireland. We also have a 3-year-old grandson and a new granddaughter. We have lived in Union Hall since we married, firstly in a rented house in Keelbeg while waiting for our own house to be built near the village.

I have been interested in the arts since childhood and I can remember constantly scribbling and drawing as a child – just give me a crayon and I'd be off. I also remember my frustrated premature attempts at trying to sharpen a pencil – I must have been about 3 years old then. When first at school, I loved the feel of chalk on the blackboard or on slate. I think I inherited creativity from my father's side. He could turn his hand to anything and manufacture farm implements from very limited raw materials. That generation were obliged to improvise and I well remember an aunt who made wonderful cushions from sacking material and bits of wool. By the age of 7 or 8, I was trying to emulate my father's creativity, for example by making a doll's house from cardboard boxes and the like. During my time in Cork I attended night classes at the Municipal School of Art and, when I moved to West Cork, I continued with art classes in Rossa College, Skibbereen. I became a member of the West Cork Arts Centre, where I befriended Ruth Holmes (a London-based batik artist) and had the privilege of working in Ruth's workshops in Leap and Kinsale.

Subsequently, I used art throughout my teaching career, for example using sketching and illustration to help a child struggling with the concept of numbers or the concept underlying a mathematical formula. In such situations, illustration can cut a bright path through the fog of theory. This applies generally, not only to children or those with dyslexia or with numeracy problems. Over the years, I've promoted the arts at school to the best of my ability. I've staged numerous dramatic productions, have written scripts for school plays and, above all, have painted stage designs. These productions have stayed in my mind over the years as I hope they have in the minds of former pupils. I particularly remember the millennium project at St Joseph's, where the 180 children and all staff had their handprints immortalised in paint. These handprints are now held in the school library and, over the years, have brought unexpected comfort to people, for example when displayed at the funerals of former pupils or staff members.

It therefore should come as no surprise to hear that I love symbolism and the creation of symbolism in my art. I have a fascination with hands, with their uniqueness, their ability to leave a 'divine' mark and to be an integral part of communication. My love of symbolism obliges me to form a relationship with my subjects and to attempt to capture the essence of a place or person – this relationship is what goes through my head as I paint. I love to deconstruct things – to pull them apart – and then perhaps focus on just one element, from which I create the bigger picture. Thus, if considering a seascape, I might be drawn to an anchor and base a painting on this. An old anchor now on display in the village once plagued local fishermen, who repeatedly got it caught in their nets and came to call it the 'Devil's Hook'. What a wonderful subject for a painting with all this history! I also have a notion to paint lighthouses, a subject that intrigues me with its symbolism – beams of hope and safety.

I paint mainly in watercolour – a medium that has an air of magic about it and that can achieve a unique sense of lucidity and light. However, it's not an easy medium and can go very wrong unless you get the consistency just right. Like many, I marvel at the talent of J.M.W. Turner and his ability to allow the paint to do the work in forming the composition. I also work a little in acrylics, which, unlike watercolour, are very forgiving and particularly suit some subjects. Painting brings me a sense of peace and I become totally lost in time and place at the easel. Over the years, I've had to balance painting with professional and domestic responsibilities. Trying to find space has been a constant problem. While the kitchen table has been put to great use, the need to tidy up afterwards is a constant frustration. Happily, work on creating a studio next to the house has now been completed. I don't know myself!

21

Freddie Sheahan-Murphy

Though christened Winifred after my mother's sister, since infancy I have been called 'Freddie'. I was brought up in the village of Leap in West Cork and was the second of Tom and Betty Sheahan's five children. My mother was a legal secretary in Skibbereen and met my father when he was doing business with his solicitor in Wolfe's offices. My parents were devoted to each other all of their married lives and there was never a cross word between them. They worked together in the business – bar, shop, Post Office, etc. – and my father enjoyed some farming. My Sheahan ancestors were from a prosperous farming family from North Cork who came to Leap around 1830. They were responsible for the building of the Catholic church, my ancestral home in the village, parish schools and, by all accounts, the building of the road between Leap and Glandore in pre-famine times. The family was well off and at one time owned several houses in Leap and land to the east and west of the village.

My parents ran a thriving guesthouse following the formation of the West Cork Accommodation Bureau by my father – the first of its kind in the area. Guests from all over Europe arrived at the Inn, including those with horse-drawn Romany caravans. It was an interesting and busy time and we kids mixed with the European children, who didn't speak English but with whom we managed to communicate quite well. All of the family helped out in the business. The fifth generation of the family is now involved. I lived in Leap until the age of fourteen, attended the local primary school, then the Convent of Mercy in Skibbereen and completed secondary school as a boarder at Drishane Convent, Millstreet. My childhood memories were very happy, except for a few horrendous years with a certain primary school teacher – so much so, that I didn't want to go to school. The psychological abuse was worse than the beatings. Those tender formative years between the ages of 6 and 9 have left an abiding unhappy memory.

Freddie Sheahan-Murphy

THE OLD PIER, UNION HALL

I drew and painted from about the age of 5. Both my mother and maternal grandmother were highly creative people and, although neither painted, they apparently thought that I had some talent and encouraged me. I was highly commended for a sunset scene that I entered in the Caltex Children's Art Competition. At boarding school, I didn't buy into the general obsession with sports and preferred to spend my time painting. I was greatly encouraged by the art teacher, Sister Mary, and received extra tuition from her outside of school hours. I loved everything connected with art – the smell of oil paint, the use of different media, the whole hands-on with canvases. I sat the Leaving Certificate at 16 and my regret is that I didn't go to full-time art college afterwards. There was no such thing as career guidance at that time and the possibility of going to art school had never entered my head.

Instead I went to St Anne's School of Home Management, Sion Hill, Dublin. There, arts and crafts as well as cooking were a major part of the curriculum and I loved it. This led to a diploma and I subsequently took on an administrative post with Guinness's at St James' Gate and worked with them for ten years. While in Dublin, I acquired a Diploma in Graphic Design and Commercial Art after two years of work. I worked to deadlines at weekends in the design and layout of advertisements. While at Guinness's, I entered an arts and crafts competition at the Rupert Guinness Hall and won first prize for a portrait painting. On moving to Cork, I had an exhibition at Allied Irish Bank, Patrick Street, which sold well and led to commissions. This was greatly encouraging.

My husband, Noel Murphy, and I married in 1975 and we have two daughters, both of whom are successful scientists. When the elder of the two was aged six months, I resigned from Guinness to be with her. Later, while the girls attended school, I worked at the Press Office in University College Cork. While there, I produced a cover illustration for a book by David Buckley on the life of the revolutionary, James Fintan Lalor. During this time, I studied life drawing and watercolour at the Crawford Municipal School of Art. Despite this formal art education, I regard myself as primarily a self-taught artist. I have been an avid collector of art books and have used these to experiment with various artistic styles. However, I try to ensure that my own style of painting is further developed without getting lost in the process. Some artists manage to replicate the same subject matter and technique over and over. That would be very uninteresting for me.

The family moved to Clonakilty, West Cork, when my husband was made a bank manager there and we lived 'over the shop' for the bones of ten years. When he was asked to move back to Cork city, he declined and decided to take early retirement, which was available then for a limited time. He never regretted that decision. He is an avid rugby enthusiast, having played at all levels, including for both Leinster and Munster. While living in Clonakilty, I had two successful solo exhibitions at Spillers Lane Gallery. Later, I was a member of the Tayt Artists' Cooperative for six years; we rented a shop space and ran it ourselves. The group also had a successful exhibition in Ardgillan Castle, Balbriggan, north Dublin. We moved back to my home village of Leap in 1999, where we had built a house, and I opened May

Early Morning, Keelbeg; pastel on Sandsfix board; 2013; 34.5 × 34.5cm.

Wind Gallery, which showcased both my own work and that of other artists. Like so many other galleries, it succumbed to the economic recession. In places like West Cork, galleries critically depend on the support of passing visitors and, of late, this support is hard to attract.

I work in pastel, oil, watercolour and acrylic. I like the technique of pointillism – the application of dots of pure colour to form an image. I'm an admirer of Seurat, Signac, Sisley and Pissarro. Some of my inspiration comes from the landscapes of my native West Cork and my travels abroad. I enjoy portrait painting and engage with unusual shapes and architecture – e.g. old doorways in Spain and Italy with peeling paint and such like. I also like creating appliqué pictures using silk material. I have a studio near my home.

It's very untidy, with tubes of paint, brushes, pens and canvases strewn everywhere. I don't allow anyone inside the door! Over the years, I've exhibited in group shows and have had several solo exhibitions. My work was approved for membership of the Pastel Society of Ireland. I'm also a member of the AIB Art Society and exhibit there annually and with the West Cork Art Society. My paintings are held in private collections worldwide.

Two years ago, following the death of my mother, I stopped painting. She was always a huge part of my life. I miss her enormously and have struggled to return to painting since her passing. The painting produced for this book is the first work that I've done in two years. I believe she may have some part in this. I'm so glad of it.

22

Harry Sherwin

I was born in 1954 at Murray Bridge, a small country town in South Australia, about an hour east of Adelaide. My father, Vernon Sherwin, was a Church of England minister and a truly extraordinary man. Born in 1894 to a naval family in Gosport, Hampshire, he came to Australia as a young man in 1913, travelling alone. He worked as a stockman, then as a missionary in northern Australia and New Guinea, where he later fought during World War II, swapping chaplaincy for a machine gun when called to join a commando unit. Some of his war memorabilia are in the Australian War Memorial in Canberra, including a set of his communion vessels and a photograph of him hoisting the regimental flag at Salamaua, New Guinea, when this was captured from the Japanese in 1943. My father was a respected anthropologist and Fellow of the Royal Society of Anthropologists (FRSA). He made language translations and documented native customs and dress using laborious wet-plate photography. My mother, Mary Morton, was third-generation Australian. Before they first met, she and my father were penfriends while she was in high school and he was a young minister in outback Australia. When they married, the young bride followed her husband to New Guinea, where they started a family before the outbreak of war. By some distance, I was the youngest in a family of four.

I had a very happy childhood. Living in Murray Bridge, on the lower reaches of the River Murray, gave me a love of water and of painting water. By my early 20s, I had bought a riverside shack, so that I have now been painting the river for over 35 years. I went to the local primary school and later spent five years as a boarder at St Peter's College, one of Adelaide's prestigious public schools for boys. That was also a wonderful experience. Following high school, at the age of 17 I studied fine art at the Torrens College of Advanced Education (now part of the University of South Australia) in Adelaide, graduating with an Advanced Diploma of Teaching (Fine Art) in 1974. Thereafter, I worked for five years as art master back at my old alma mater, St Peter's College. I resigned from this job in 1980 so that I could devote more time to art. I continue to teach part-time and enjoy conducting workshops for mature students.

I met my partner, Llewena Llewellyn, at Port

The Cottage, Union Hall; oil on board; 1995; 25 × 45.5cm.

Elliot, a delightful seaside town at the southern tip of the Fleurieu Peninsula, south of Adelaide. Llewena has family connections in the Clare Valley and, around 1990, we moved to Watervale. This is a town of about 200 people right in the middle of the Clare Valley, which is itself named after County Clare in Ireland. The region is particularly noted for the production of some of Australia's best wines – especially Riesling. We live in a lovely cottage surrounded by vineyards and I have a studio attached to the house.

I consider myself a realist painter, although the term takes no account of my deep regard for abstraction and collage. My main body of work is figurative and I like to paint directly from the subject. I am most at home painting *en plein air*. This can be something of a challenge in Australia, particularly when you have to contend with dust and flies. I also enjoy studio-based work and some of the work for which I am best known (e.g. my crowd scenes) has been studio-based from beginning to end. I am equally enamoured of oil, watercolour and gouache. I once worked in acrylics, but quickly dumped these for oils because of the greater possibilities offered by oil. Nowadays, whenever I use acrylics it is mainly for preliminary studies. Still-life subjects, interiors, portraiture and the figure all have their place in my exhibited work; indeed, the subject of a painting is but one component of the artistic experience. Technique provides the fuel. I also believe that the composition of a painting trumps its subject when it comes to aesthetic appreciation.

Regarding technique, I am not a fan of photo - realism. For me, brush strokes are all-important – they are what give a painting its life, its physicality, its sense of lyricism and its pulse. For the artist, brush strokes are a kind of signature and, like handwriting, make a work of art unique. Regarding subject matter, I particularly like painting translucent subjects such as glass and water. The transference of light also greatly interests me. Over the years, I have been greatly attracted to the Impressionists, the Post-Impressionists and the Cubists. I particularly admire the work of Cézanne, Matisse, Braque and Picasso.

My painting of Union Hall in this book dates from 1995, when I spent some months travelling in Europe as part of a study award and spent three memorable weeks right by the pier at Keelbeg with Llewena and her mother – another Llewena. It's hard to believe that this is now almost twenty years ago. This was a boom time in Ireland, with new houses going up everywhere. All five pubs in the village were thriving. The local football team had just won some championship or other and I remember drinking long and hard from the cup. The weather was great and I got a lot of work done. I came to Union Hall from Edinburgh, where I'd been confined to painting in a studio. It was just great to be able to work outdoors in West Cork. I painted pretty well all of the time; I really couldn't stop, as the scenery kept jumping out at me just asking to be painted. I completed over a dozen paintings, all of which sold as soon as I brought them back to Adelaide. I remember wishing that I'd given Edinburgh a skip and spent more time in Union Hall. I'd jump at the chance of coming back if the opportunity ever arose. Like 120% of the world, I've got some Irish ancestry and I have got a real affinity for Ireland. I love its wildness and the poetic side – the lyricism – of life there.

My only regret from my time in Ireland in 1995 is that I didn't manage to catch up with some old friends – the late and great Noel Sheridan and his equally amazing wife, Liz. I first met Noel in the 1970s in Adelaide, where he had set up the city's Experimental Art Foundation. He had immense energy and vision and the ability to solve any problem. The Foundation survived on a trickle of funding and one time was down to its last $100 or so. Noel gambled everything on a horse running at Cheltenham and nobody was in the least surprised when it romped home at long odds. Noel and Liz were loved by all who knew them and left a legacy in the large number of artists they had nurtured. Noel later became the Director of the National College of Art and Design in Dublin, which he successfully steered through some challenging times.

I have exhibited my work from an early age and am currently working towards my 33rd solo exhibition. I mainly exhibit in Adelaide and Sydney, and of course locally in the Clare Valley and in other parts of South Australia. Over the years, I have received numerous awards, including the highly prestigious Heysen Art Prize, which I have won on two occasions, in 1985 and 2011. I have undertaken commissions for the Government of New South Wales and in 2012 this state government sponsored a Survey Exhibition of my work in the city of Orange, a retrospective exhibition that featured 48 works (still-life paintings, landscapes in the *plein air* tradition, collages, crowd themes and studio works) that I had painted over a 32-year period from 1980. Aside from Australia, my paintings have made their way into private collections in various parts of Europe and North America.

My career as a painter has provided me with opportunities to travel and, at different times, I have gone to paint in such places as Ireland, Scotland, England, Italy, Greece, Turkey, Egypt and Thailand. Finally, I feel really honoured to know that my painting of Union Hall from all those years ago has become the prompt for this book.

23

Martin Stone

I was born in Cardiff, Wales, and brought up in the Tiger Bay area of the city. I am of Jamaican and Welsh ancestry and the youngest of ten children. My father, Cleveland George Stone, came to England from Jamaica to join the Royal Air Force at the start of World War II. He had notions of becoming a pilot but quickly learned that his racial background pretty much excluded him from this. During the war, he was posted to South Wales and there he met and married my mother, Muriel Norton. After the war, my father worked as a postman and my mother as a nurse. Interracial marriages were not well accepted in Cardiff in the late 1940s, but my parents found a haven in Tiger Bay (since immortalised by the singer Shirley Bassey); this is where local families of mixed race often ended up. Four of my five brothers and my four sisters still live in the Cardiff area. My eldest brother Johnny, who died in the late 1980s, was quite a character and is still remembered around the Tiger Bay area.

I went to school locally in Cardiff and later in Dinas Powys on the outskirts of the city. I didn't do particularly well at school but was always good at art-related subjects. At that time, I was particularly attracted to sculpture and pottery. I wasn't particularly interested in the way the school taught painting and was told by my art teacher that I would never make a living as a painter. After I finished secondary school, I worked at a number of jobs: shop work, office work, whatever work I could get my hands on really. At the age of 20, I went to the Cardiff College of Art and progressed from there to the Birmingham College of Art. The Birmingham College was housed in a fantastic Venetian-style redbrick building right in the city centre and next door to a horrendous office block. I spent three years there learning in the old-fashioned 'academic' tradition, which I feel has served me

Untitled; oil on canvas; 2010; 59 × 78cm.

well. A couple of years later, I studied for my MA at the famous Chelsea College of Art in London – another great experience.

Throughout this time, I did some mural work and community-based artwork to support myself in London and in South Wales. For example, I was involved in the construction of a 200-acre sculpture garden and arts complex on the site of an old coalmine in Caerphilly, near Cardiff. I met my wife Anne O'Driscoll in London in the early 1990s. Anne is originally from Skibbereen and I began to visit Skibb with her on a regular basis. From the start we were very keen to move to Skibbereen but the cost of living in Ireland at that time was prohibitive for us. Instead, we moved to Cardiff and used this as a stepping-stone on our way back to West Cork. At one stage we thought long and hard about moving to Australia, went through the immigration process and even got ourselves visas. However, one visit to Australia in the late 1990s convinced us that West Cork was where we really wanted to live.

We moved to Skibbereen in 2003. I set up a small studio in Townshend Street and started to exhibit at local galleries. To begin with, I wasn't able to fully support myself and my family through art and so I also worked on a range of community projects in Cork city. I became a full-time artist in about 2005. I now mostly work from a studio at my home in Skibbereen. Anne and I have two children – Niamh (b. 2000) and Konrad (b. 2003).

Essentially, I see myself as an abstract painter, though much of my work is figurative. I try to paint what I know and the things with which I can make an emotional connection. I fell in love with the landscape of West Cork some twenty years ago and, since then, its varying textures have never ceased to inspire me – in particular the sea, lakes, fields and mountains. The kaleidoscope of colour reminds me of Gauguin's assertion that, for the artist, colour has its own meaning. I also love the architecture of West Cork and the rich primary colours in which houses here are often painted. This contrasts with parts of Wales where I have lived and where local by-laws oblige people to paint their houses in a range of similar and often drab colours.

I like to have a lot of diversity in my work and tend to get bored if I'm working on the same subject or theme for a while. This means that, if I'm working on landscapes or on still lifes, for example, after a while I move on to painting people. I hate the idea of getting stuck in a rut. I know that other painters focus on one thing and stay with it, but I'm not like that. While I like pretty much all artistic media, I particularly love oil. For me, there is nothing quite like it; it has a life. Oil of course is difficult to manipulate and it takes time to dry, but these are small prices to pay. I also like painting in watercolour and gouache. Acrylic is OK but is my least favourite medium and doesn't feel alive like oil paint. I draw all of the time and love drawing in pen and ink. When building up a painting, I often (but not always) draw the subject first and then overpaint on the drawing. I often work on two or three versions of the same subject at a time, moving from one version to the next, building up one element to see how it will work while trying not to lose the elements that are worth retaining. I mostly paint in natural light and don't like painting in the evenings – I draw then instead.

I'm quite a prolific worker and feel the need to paint every day. I think I'm a bit like a footballer who needs to stay 'match-fit' to retain his competitive edge. Painting every day allows me to maintain my 'art-fitness'. I often disappear into the studio for hours at a time and get totally lost in my work. In some ways, I never really leave the studio – I even have a drawing/sketching area in the kitchen at home, where I sometimes work instead of going next door to my proper studio. I take a couple of weeks' holiday each year, but even then – and to the disgust of my wife and kids – take my sketch pads with me. For me, art is like an addiction or an obsession, but it's too late to worry about this now. It defines me and I just have to do it.

Over the past ten years or so, I have become more professional as a painter. By this I mean that I am now more disciplined, am able to build up a body of work for exhibition and am better able to meet deadlines. I am more confident about my artistic ability and am getting better at promoting myself and my work. Until now, and for various reasons, I have mainly regarded myself as a West Cork artist and have focused on exhibiting my work locally and in Cork city. I am now looking to the national stage and had my first solo exhibition in Dublin in early 2013.

24

Donald Teskey RHA

*Photograph by
Paddy Benson*

My Teskey ancestors were Palatines who came to West Limerick around 300 years ago, from the banks of the Rhine, to escape religious persecution by the French. They were farmers and wine-makers and, unlike those who went to America and fell upon hard times, Palatines in Ireland prospered and integrated well. Through industry and ingenuity they made a significant contribution to the advancement of farming and farm management. They substituted cider-making for wine-making

and were reputedly hard-drinking until converted to Methodism and sobriety by John Wesley in the 18th century. I was brought up in the townland of Castle Matrix on the outskirts of Rathkeale in a wonderful old Palatine cottage. I was the second youngest and the only male in a family of four. My mother, Maureen Hudson, also had Palatine origins and also came from the locality. Her family were shopkeepers. My father, Norman Teskey, was a joiner, who, with his brother and father, built up the once-prominent building firm J.H. Teskey & Sons. Unfortunately, the business succumbed to an economic recession in the 1970s, an event that was particularly traumatic for my father.

I went to national school in Rathkeale and then boarded at Wesley College in Dublin. Creativity was always encouraged at home. My father was as much an engineer as a joiner, was highly practical and could find a solution to every mechanical problem. He was forever inventing his own tools and machines. He was a lover of nature and the outdoors and had a keen interest in photography, with a darkroom for developing black-and-white photographs. I drew from a young age and remember getting praise for my drawing in primary school. My parents recognised and nurtured this talent, buying me art materials. I still have some sketches from fishing trips with my father, when I would draw as much as fish. While much of this was intuitive, I also read books on how to paint, how to draw, how to mix colours and the like. I was intrigued by the possibilities and I

Untitled; acrylic on paper; 2012; 19 × 24.5cm.

experimented a great deal with materials from my father's workshop.

I studied at Limerick School of Art and Design. I was part of the second intake into the NCEA course at Limerick; Charlie Harper was on the staff and Jack Donovan was still the school head. Some of the best contemporary artists – people like Charlie Tyrrell and Barrie Cooke – served as visiting lecturers. Art college teaching of that period was beginning to move more towards conceptual art, in line with other European colleges, with the emphasis away from the academic ability to draw, so it fell to the students at Limerick to club together to maintain a strong culture of drawing in the college. I was able to put myself through college through earnings from summer work, for example spending one summer picking tobacco in Ontario, Canada. It was hellish work, but the money was great. For a number of summers I was able to spend time in New York City, where I got to see so much great art.

I graduated with a Diploma in Fine Art in 1978 and stayed in Limerick for a year before moving back to Dublin, where I had many friends. I was introduced to the Lincoln Gallery on Lincoln Place, which provided a platform for many young as well as established artists. I had begun working on a series of surrealist drawings exploring the urban landscape. I wasn't painting at this point, so I was thrilled to be offered a solo show of my drawings at the Lincoln Gallery for the following year. The show was well received by the critics and, to my amazement, sold very well. I showed several times with the Lincoln Gallery before it closed in the mid-1980s, the director Blaithín de Sachy moving on to become the Director of the Hendricks Gallery. During that time I participated in GPA awards and was selected for an exhibition of contemporary Irish art curated by the American writer and art critic Lucy Lippard. This toured several major US cities over a three-year period before returning to the Douglas Hyde Gallery at Trinity College. It included a broad range of contemporary practice by leading artists from the island of Ireland. I began working at the College of Marketing and Design (now part of Dublin Institute of Technology), where I taught drawing in the Fine Art and Design departments.

By the end of the 1980s I felt I had exhausted the drawing process as a primary medium and began the transition to painting. Returning to painting after ten years of drawing required almost a complete unlearning of everything I had done previously in order to find the means to bring real expression to my painting. I avoided using paintbrushes, instead using other 'mark-making tools' such as plastering trowels, palette knives and sticks. It is essential for me that the energy and the physicality of the painting process be communicated through the mark that the artist puts on canvas. My first solo exhibition of paintings was with Dublin's Rubicon Gallery in 1993. The exhibition was both well received by the critics and a sell-out. I quickly evolved into painting on a big scale, with urban landscapes as my main subject matter.

In 1996 I was awarded a Fellowship by the Ballinglen Arts Foundation on the west coast of Mayo. Though just newly established, Ballinglen was beginning to attract international artists, mostly on two-month residencies. The area is remote, with a unique coastline and with an air of melancholy, perhaps explained by its long history of emigration. Unlike West Cork, Kerry or Connemara, it has an elemental rather than a spectacular beauty and this only reveals itself slowly, so that one needs to spend time there. I've since returned many times. At first, I didn't consider the sea as a subject. Instead, I was fascinated by the villages and farm buildings in the landscape. That's what I painted. On later visits, I started to really look at the coastline and gradually it began to reveal itself as a subject. In the process, I had to overcome the challenge of experiencing the seascape without being overwhelmed by it.

Through my Mayo paintings in particular, I've tried to convey the experience of being immersed in a landscape. As a result of the Ballinglen Fellowship, I was encouraged to spend time in other parts of Ireland to explore areas previously unknown to me. For example, I spent a couple of weeks with Margaret Warren in Castletownshend in 1998, with the boathouse as my studio. It was during this time that I first encountered the villages of Union Hall and Baltimore. I continue to be fascinated by Irish coastal villages, particularly in winter, and by the architecture and various aspects of harbour communities. The role of the artist residency as a place of retreat is hugely significant for many artists in developing new work. In recent years I worked at the Vermont Studio Centre in Vermont, the Joseph and Annie Albers Foundation in Connecticut and the Centre Culturel Irlandais in Paris. These are all very different environments from the west coast of Ireland but were equally challenging and hugely rewarding experiences.

I was elected a full member of the Royal Hibernian Academy in 2003, at a time when the organisation was undergoing a process of revitalisation. In the years since, the Academy has gone from strength to strength, with its fantastic city-centre exhibition space. My current role as Keeper of the Academy is to oversee the Academy's permanent collection and to serve on the Council. I was elected a member of Aosdána in 2006. I've had numerous solo exhibitions in Ireland and the UK and my work has been exhibited in group shows throughout the UK, the USA, Canada, China, South Africa, France and Germany. My work is in many private, corporate and state collections both here and abroad.

Note: The above text was put together based on a series of conversations between the artist and Paul and Aileen in December 2012.

25

Christine Thery

of prohibition. Hans' wife, Minna Thomas, was from Welsh farming stock. My mother, Irene Nagursky, was of Russian and Polish extraction and was born in Harbin, Manchuria, but with her mother and grandmother was displaced to Shanghai by the Japanese. They were in a perilous position as stateless refugees – despised by both Europeans and Chinese and hoping to be offered a home in a friendly country. My father came to Shanghai to help evacuate refugees before the imminent arrival of the Communists. He and my mother met, fell in love and married within weeks and so she got her ticket out in the best way possible. Her mother and grandmother left soon after, moving to Australia. Another branch of the family settled in America.

My parents first lived in the Philippines and then Hong Kong, where I went to school but learned nothing. Despite living on such an exciting and exotic island, we had not one lesson in the Chinese language or culture, instead following an alien and boring English curriculum. Ten wasted years! My dislike of the cruel imprisonment of children in schools stems from those awful days. Outside of school, life was good. We were free to play outdoors and weekends were spent on boats, by the pool or at the beach.

My education began after I left school and discovered books. When I was 19 my father retired to Vancouver, but my parents weren't happy there so we moved to England. An A level in Art got me into Plymouth Pre Dip, a dream come true as I'd

O ver half a century ago in Hong Kong, during a typhoon, my twin sister and I were born. Stella, the older by fifteen minutes, now lives near Schull, where she has a successful and stylish shop. Our younger sister, Diana, lives in Cornwall. We have a complicated genealogy. My father, Clifford Jean Baptiste Thery, was born in Canada. His father, Hans, was a German hotel owner of French descent who offered sanctuary to thirsty Americans in the days

Paul, His Father and Australia; oil on canvas; 2009; 50 × 75cm.

always had a passion for drawing and hated my few attempts at menial office jobs. I didn't care about the art degree and still can't see any benefit in having one. However, college meant four years of freedom to explore an exciting path. One year in Plymouth led to a further three in the Sculpture Department at Winchester, where I also did printmaking and photography, hiding in the darkroom to escape those tutors who pushed us in unwelcome directions. Enlightenment came from a realisation that the tutors' work (which we rarely saw) was no less full of faults or open to criticism than that of their students! After Winchester, I turned down the offer of further art study in London. I had saved to go 'home' to Hong Kong on the Trans-Siberian railway by working weekends and evenings as a hospital cleaner. This was one of the best jobs I've ever had, as cleaners served the food and chatted to and cheered up the patients – the nurses had to do the dirty work!

Back in Hong Kong, I neither wanted nor could afford an 'ex-pat' lifestyle and chose to live on the small nearby island of Cheung Chau – a car-free place inhabited by fishing people, farmers and foreigners like myself. It was an exciting place to live. I got a job in the extramural art department of Hong Kong University, but I soon realised that this kept me from what I most wanted to do – my drawing and photography. Setting up as a penniless freelance illustrator and photographer was hard. I lived off muesli and noodles from market stalls while most of my earnings went on rent. Getting very thin and starting to lose my hair made me realise, but not regret, the downside of my chosen life. Gradually I got work, selling drawings and mixed-media pictures.

After some years on Cheung Chau and a brief attempt at living back in England, I moved to the neighbouring island of Lantau – a tropical paradise alive with the richest flora and fauna imaginable. Though bigger than Hong Kong Island, it was sparsely inhabited by farmers, with scattered fishing villages and romantic monasteries and convents on wooded hillsides. I lived in a traditional village helping to set up an agricultural project growing traditional crops organically. I drew, photographed and recorded the village life of one of the last traditional farming areas of South China. Such people are disappearing all over the world, as the small get swallowed up by the big and the loud. These are the same kind of people that you still find in parts of Europe or south-west Ireland. They could exchange the same life stories if only they had a common language. What I enjoy is doing some translation in the form of printmaking, drawings or paintings – the language of pictures. Pretentious-sounding maybe but true! When a new Hong Kong airport was planned for Lantau, with a bridge, turning it into a 'non-island' and bringing in a flood of people from Hong Kong, I knew it was time to leave.

After a few years back in England, when I did more and more etching, I married Gubby Williams and we moved onto *Minstrel*, the gaff cutter he had built. I took my small press aboard – into the (always dry) bilge – and we set off for Ireland, the first stop on Gubby's long-planned voyage. An exciting five years began then, ending in south-west Ireland when we finally settled on Heir Island, with its strong echoes of the islands of Hong Kong. We had discovered the island by chance on our first trip and bought a two-acre plot on our return. Our voyage had taken us down the coast of France to Spain and Portugal, the Canaries, across the bleak and lonely Atlantic to the Caribbean, the Bahamas and up the intracoastal waterway to Maine. There, we spent two winters ashore in the snow and ice, where Gubby worked in the Brooklyn Boat Yard and I did my printmaking.

Finally, back on Heir Island, we rented a house until we sold the boat and could afford to build a house of our own (my first real home). I began painting as well as etching, and built a beautiful studio. We grew all our own vegetables and had chickens and ducks. The vegetable patch shrank when I began having a show each summer and spring became a time for developing paintings not beans. We still grow our own potatoes, using lots of seaweed. I now rarely etch, as painting, with all its demands, has taken over my life. I have a one-person show most years in the Morris Gallery in Skibbereen and sell paintings in other galleries and from my studio. I work exclusively in oils,

loving the way they behave, and, like many representational painters, I am always in search of the more free and abstract. There are some completely abstract paintings that I love, but I can't seem to do them myself, always needing some reality as at least a starting-point.

It's easy to sound pretentious and paintings should speak for themselves. There is too much said it seems about things that are, after all, just pictures for walls! And can you trust the wisdom of people who spend their lives painting pictures? I paint over more paintings than I finish. I usually prefer my charcoal drawings — normally the starting-point of my paintings. I use photography but don't copy photographs. Paintings usually begin full of hope then become exciting and reach a plateau of ordinariness before the inevitable disappointment. I think this is the same for most painters and is what keeps us trying for the unachievable masterpiece! I rarely like my older paintings and would probably paint over the picture in this book if it were still in my studio!